MW01012420

Eighter from Decatur

Eighter from Decatur

GROWING UP IN NORTH TEXAS

>—•—<

by Jim Tom Barton

Foreword by Joe B. Frantz

TEXAS A&M UNIVERSITY PRESS

College Station and London

Library of Congress Cataloging in Publication Data

Barton, Jim Tom, 1910–
    Eighter from Decatur.

    Bibliography: p.
    Includes index.
    1. Barton, Jim Tom, 1910– 2. Decatur, Tex.— Biography.
3. Decatur, Tex.—Social life and customs.
I. Title.
F394.D259B373   976.4'532   79-5279
ISBN 0-89096-089-5

Manufactured in the United States of America
FIRST EDITION

To

Uncle Carl Sterling Perrin
a man with a remarkable memory

Contents

List of Illustrations

Foreword

People with small-town backgrounds generally divide into two groups: those who sentimentalize until they blot out all reality inconsistent with nostalgia and those who criticize their small towns as oppressive, restricting, devoid of tolerance for creativity, and nosy to the point of outlawing privacy and individuality. Small-town life lies somewhere between Thornton Wilder's *Our Town*, which traces the comfortable experience of people living with people who know and trust each other, and Sinclair Lewis' *Main Street*, which exposes the shallow and small minds that pose as people.

Like Jim Tom Barton, I belong somewhere in the middle. My small town, another county seat only slightly larger than Decatur, was Weatherford, also an enormous thirty miles from Fort Worth, which represented sophistication and wealth and sin. My father was an immigrant Illini from a Dutch-German community that just missed being incestuous. My grandmother was a Brubaker who married a Frantz. In turn one of her daughters married a Brubaker, and her child married my mother's oldest brother, a Buckley, after my mother got those two families introduced. My mother's cousin married my Dad's next older brother. And so it went.

As they grew older, many of them sold their eighty-acre farms in central Illinois and migrated to southern California to escape the rigorous winters. Practicing a religion that inveighed against owing another man (a tenet I have not held to), they took their money in cash. Some of them invested in orange groves. As many bought gold stock, for though they would wear no gold around their necks or on their bodies, they respected money. Those who bought rocky land eventually prospered; the stock of the others proved mostly worthless, and so they eked out a life waiting for an afterlife, in which again they could tread the streets of gold. Gold loomed large in their thinking.

Mother was of a different stripe. She was born on a farm southwest of Weatherford in 1876 of parents who had come from Kentucky and Illinois. She grew up a fearful woman, nurtured by every old wives' tale that Parker County could produce. When my sisters had reached adulthood, she still refused to let them drive alone to Fort Worth for fear some white slaver would stick a needle in them and drop them through a trap door while they were drugged; they would then be chuted off into a life worse than death (a sort of Victorian version of "I'd rather be dead than Red"). But though she feared men and their bestial appetites, she surrounded herself with boys. Her favorite stricture was that women were put on this earth to "accommodate" men. She boasted to me that she was married for six weeks before she let my father touch her. I believe her.

So I grew up, the son of farm parents, who undoubtedly knew all the facts of life from bulls and cows or dogs and cats and chickens. But the only indication I received that s-e-x was a natural occurrence between the two genders was from other boys, who made it sound even dirtier than Mother did.

The main problem with small towns is the lack of privacy. Everyone watches you strain and grow. If you make a mistake, it's all over town by morning. Now it's forty years since I left Weatherford, but I can tell you just about every peccadillo committed by every man, woman, and child in the 1930's, not to mention a lot that came down in the town's folklore from all the way back to the previous century. Looking back, I know I must have longed for an anonymity that I didn't even know existed. Just to find out things for myself. Just to overreach without someone reporting to my aunt, who was promptly on the phone to my mother, "Did you know that Joe just . . . ?"

At one time I counted. I was related to fifty-eight people in the community. Fred M. is thirty minutes late getting back from Fort Worth: "What could he have been up to?" Anita S. has worked late for three straight nights at the bank: "Is she trying to break up X's marriage?" Gossip flowed like wine, which is not an apt figure, since most Weatherford people never saw wine except at communion—and usually it was grape juice, except at the Presbyterian and Episcopal churches.

The town worried whether the Methodist presiding elder cheated on his golf scores, whether the Episcopalian rector sneaked off to Fort Worth to attend moving picture shows (after all, the Episcopalians didn't have Sunday night services, and he had once been seen heading east in his car toward the edge of town), whether the Baptist minister was smiling at one of the widows in his congregation, or why the Presbyterian minister read his sermons. The concept of a proper preacher was the man who just put his head back and roared the words that God placed in his mouth. We also preferred that he be specific about sins—dancing, drinking, roadhouses, saxophones and jazz, high school petting, contract bridge. Then we could sit back and speculate about whom he was preaching at, which gave us a topic for another week.

It is difficult to overestimate the role of the church in such a turned-in society. The church provided nearly the only entertainment we had that was not illicit. You had Sunday school, morning worship, B.Y.P.U. (Baptist Young People's Union, which was later changed when some of the conservative fathers downstate objected to using *union* in an approving sense), Christian Endeavor, Epworth League, and Sunday night service. Then prayer meeting on Wednesday night and choir practice on Thursday. In between, the various women's groups met, the young people held parties, and in high school Monday morning was partially devoted to chapel. Even if you were a heathen Chinee, you couldn't escape the all-consuming maw of the church.

And yet the woman generally acknowledged as the best primary-grades teacher in Weatherford was an open atheist, and the town swore by her. The doctors universally stayed away from church, and the town forgave them. Even my mother, with her irrational fears, went off to Illinois with the local Jewish merchant when he made his annual buying trip to Chicago. For two days and two nights she rode the train with him—and she was afraid to let her daughters go off to Fort Worth alone together in their own car. I am not astonished at my grandmother, who was fat and jolly and forward-looking, but I haven't been able to explain my mother at all. Her fear that when you left home you would get into things was well founded, though, for she fell in love with my father while in Illinois, married him, and brought him back to Texas in 1900. After I came along nearly two decades later, she spent a lot of my time telling me, "You know, Northern men are different." I have observed them ever since, physically and spiritually and socially, and I still don't know how they differ.

Why all of this personal reminiscence? Because Jim Tom Barton's book will cause memories to well up, memories that have long lain dormant. Barton has given me a new hero in Orus Mooney, who dared to question the values of Decatur and Wise County. A young farmer was threatened with expulsion from the local church for giving a ride to town to a young lady of questionable virtue. Perhaps, the town murmured, he made an indecent suggestion during the ride. Mooney, a local schoolteacher and Sunday school teacher, withdrew his letter from the church in protest against the violation of the Biblical injunction forbidding judgments. Fifty years later, says Barton, Mooney still has not rejoined the church, although the farmer, now an old farmer, remains a member. Mooney's action required the same kind of courage as being a liberal Democrat in Odessa, Texas.

The book is filled with such vignettes. But it is more than vignettes. Barton is especially effective in his descriptions of how things get done. After having read his book, a person from the sixteenth century or the 1960's could drop in on Barton's Decatur and know how to put together a homemade kite, how to play wolf-over-the-river, why a farmer ought to keep a dog, and where to buy bootleg whiskey. I know now why we always stopped outside the gate of a farmhouse and, if no one was outside to greet us, called, "Anybody home?" Like Barton's people, we never went to the front door, but I didn't know why until now.

On the whole, Barton's Decatur was a little like my own experience with Weatherford. We both were comfortable kids with no regimentation and no duties except to show up for meals. I was hungry for reading matter in a town with no library, and I read everything in the house and everything I could borrow. Once one of my uncles, who otherwise was a favorite of mine, told my mother that if she let me continue to read it would ruin me. While Mother was strict, she brooked no advice from relatives or outsiders. So I read on.

To both Barton and me, Fort Worth was the ultimate city, because we had never seen anything larger. Neither had most Weatherfordians, except maybe for an adventure at the the State Fair in Dallas. Our hometown was where the action was, and the word *action* should really be placed in quotation marks. All I needed to do was not get in the way. One of my close playmates in my early years was a black lad named Charles Fred, with whom I got along famously until one day I tried to baptize him with the garden hose and wound up putting the living room under several inches of water. Years went by, and the two of us went our own ways. But then one day when I was about sixteen my sister Ruby, pointing out a lithe black teenager on the sidewalk outside Renfro's drugstore on the square, said, "Isn't that Charles Fred?" I hopped out of the car.

"Charles Fred?" I called tentatively.

He looked perplexed, but nodded.

"Joe. Joe Frantz," I told him.

Then came a big, affectionate grin, and we hugged like two old soldiers.

Fifteen minutes later I drove up in my driveway. My mother met me at the door. "You hugged Charles Fred down on the square," she said.

Aside from my perpetual annoyance with the swiftness of non-news in Weatherford, I felt challenged. "I was glad to see him," I said, a little truculently.

"Some people in town don't take kindly to your hugging a Negro boy in public," Mother said.

"But I told you I was glad to see him."

"Don't do it anymore," said Mother, who I always suspected felt more comfortable with Negroes than she did with town whites. "It's just not done."

So the small town goes on. Weatherford has become a Fort Worth bedroom and has lost much of its identity. I suspect the same thing has happened to Decatur. But there existed a time when these county seats in rural areas were the whole world to several thousand people. They were in their ways capitals as surely as Vaduz in Liechtenstein or Andorra la Vella in Andorra. They had their semirigid social structure, and young people did not date outside their class. They had their ghettos, determined in both towns by the railroad tracks. People on the "proper side" of the tracks might have friends on the other side, but they did not really mix. Many a North Side mother must have worried herself sick about the boy from the other side who was dating her daughter. He was "bound to be up to no good, or he wouldn't be coming over here." Her only consolation, and it was a cold one, was that another mother on the South Side was equally scared that her dear boy would get "trapped."

The dismal town can provide a corrosive situation, bleak and uninviting to anyone sensitive and creative. It can produce a warm situation if you're naturally gregarious and want to know everyone you meet and if all you seek is to grow up, get a job, get married, have babies, and grow older. As President Lyndon B. Johnson liked to say, it's a place where people visit you when you're sick and care when you die.

To my mind, small-town life is overrated unless you are willing to let others make your life for you. Its chief virtue is security and sanctuary. It can be a good place to dream when you're young, though your dreams are hamstrung by the shortage of people of broad knowledge who can introduce you to good literature, to good music, to plays and art, to museums, to taste and elegance and good dining. Most of the things I have enjoyed for the past forty years, I never heard of until I left Weatherford. My body and my emotions loved the town; my mind and my soul starved for things unknown and unheard of.

Is it the same in 1980? Or has television simply replaced the gossip line? I don't know, can't know, without moving back. And that I am not about to do.

But don't let me act like a small-town arbiter. Read this book for an astringent view of small-town life in the 1920's and make up your own mind. It's a book that will make you want to read parts aloud to your partner, and it's a book that will remind you that people remain the same.

JOE B. FRANTZ
Austin, Texas

Preface

In *Eighter from Decatur* I want to provide an understanding of some of the attitudes and conditions that prevailed in a small North Texas town and its surrounding countryside during the first decades of the twentieth century. Historical information, family happenings, gossip, newspaper stories, and yarns are mingled in an effort to attain this purpose.

The yarns are either true or have been told for the truth. They include episodes in which I was involved plus stories heard from others; some are firsthand accounts and others hearsay. Some characters are real, and others fictitious. If these stories are not Texana now, I hope they will become Texana with the passage of time.

I am grateful to the late Harry H. Ransom, chancellor emeritus of the University of Texas, for encouragement and consideration. Prior to his death, he read some of the following material and suggested that I continue my writing efforts.

Joe B. Frantz, professor of history at the University of Texas, read the material and made crucial suggestions about publication. The late Roscoe C. Martin, first director of the Bureau of Municipal Research of the University of Texas in the 1930's, gave me training in writing technical reports, for which I am thankful. Elizabeth A. H. John, historian and author, volunteered encouragement and assistance.

My brother, Henry Will, retired professor of English at Midwestern State University, participated in many of the happenings and made a critique of the first draft. Orus M. Mooney, my classmate in Decatur High School and cherished friend in later life, suggested a number of anecdotes, read the manuscript, and made helpful suggestions.

Uncle Carl S. Perrin is a farmer and rancher who has been successful throughout the agricultural revolution of the twentieth century, having progressed from a pioneer-type subsistence operation in Wise County, Texas, to large-scale, mechanized wheat and cattle production on the High Plains of that state. Uncle Carl's vivid memory was an irreplaceable resource concerning family history.

My "office partner" Will Wilson, who has served both as attorney general and as justice of the supreme court of the State of Texas, helped by reviewing the manuscript and offering comments.

Others to whom I am deeply indebted include Hallie, my wife and editor. Dr. John A. Boston, psychiatrist, read much of the material and offered suggestions; Sander W. Shapiro, attorney, asked me to continue writing; and Jack A. Maguire, director of the Institute of Texan Cultures, encouraged me to write. Mrs. Harwell Hamilton Harris gave me valuable instructions; Weldon and Anita Brewer were helpful in matters of form; and Jack C. Robertson, associate professor of accounting at the University of Texas, provided inspiration.

Hiram Monroe Helm, a native of Wise County and longtime respected businessman of Decatur, has in recent years demonstrated artistic talent by drawing excellent pictures of historic and unusual buildings. He has kindly authorized the use of some of his drawings in this publication. He also helped with the text by obtaining information about events that occurred early in this century.

The late Cliff D. Cates, a lifetime resident of Decatur, published the *Pioneer History of Wise County* in 1907. Information about early settlers, many of whom Mr. Cates knew personally, would now be lost had it not been for his work and dedication. The book, reprinted in recent years by the Wise County Historical Society, is sold by that organization. Much of the information on the early pioneers in chapter 1 came from the *Pioneer History of Wise County*.

Eighter
from
Decatur

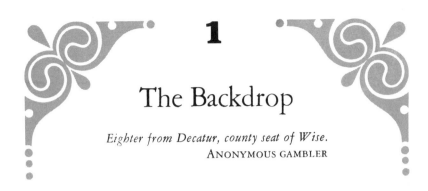

1

The Backdrop

Eighter from Decatur, county seat of Wise.
ANONYMOUS GAMBLER

Pioneers came late into the land along the border of Indian Territory because the Indians maintained a state of warfare. No equivalent of the Geneva Convention was observed by either the Indians or the settlers.

Tennessean Sam Woody traveled upstream along the Trinity River from Fort Worth in the fall of 1853 and discovered a small, fertile valley in the southeast part of what later became Wise County. In April of 1854 Woody returned to the valley with his family to find Tom McCarroll living there in a lean-to. The Woody family then traveled north a few miles and, locating another little valley, built the first cabin in the area of Wise County. Their small log structure stood many years.

Mr. Woody later told Cliff Cates, who was writing his *Pioneer History of Wise County*: "It was easy to live in those days. Sow five or six acres of wheat and it would often produce fifty bushels to the acre; cut it with a cradle, tramp and fan it out, then once or twice a year load up a wagon to which five or six steers were hitched, and after a week's trip to Dallas you would have enough to give bread to your own family and some to the neighbors for a number of weeks, until it would be the turn of someone else to make the trip. Hogs would get so fat on acorns they couldn't walk."

Shortly after Mr. Woody finished his cabin, other families moved into the area, including the Perrins from Crab Orchard, Kentucky. That family spent 1853 on good black land in Collin County and then moved west to the Wise County area, having heard that the land was fertile and covered with grass longer than the legs of a

[3]

horse. James Perrin, my grandfather, then sixteen years old, was with the family.

Indians raids subsided, and pioneer immigration continued until 1859, when Comanche Indians were blamed for killing the Mason and Cameron families on Lost Creek and also for killing a group of Delaware Indians who were friendly with the settlers. The settlers also did their share of killing.

Immigrants who arrived during the five years between 1854 and 1859 had names like Woody, McCarroll, Perrin, Brooks, Butler, Calhoun, Standifer, Ward, Boyd, Cates, Renshaw, Pickett, Shoemaker, Birdwell, White, and Halsell. Although a few came from the North, most came from Tennessee, Kentucky, Missouri, and the Old South. They were descendants of families who had moved westward with the frontier from Virginia and the Carolinas during the preceding hundred years or more. Most were self-reliant farmers, well acquainted with hardship. If they had a specialty, it was pioneering.

Some were of German or Huguenot heritage, but the ancestors of most came from the British Isles. Many called themselves Scotch-Irish. The immigrants wanted churches, schools, and better lives for their children. The settlers were loyal to the South even though they did not come from a Southern-plantation background and owned very few slaves.

Before the boundaries of Wise County were surveyed, Daniel Howell of Denton decided to open a store in the new community. He wanted to locate in whatever would someday be the county seat. Mr. Howell computed the center of Wise County by making projections based on the Denton and Cooke county lines. When he visited the point he had calculated, he was below a hill where the Grand Prairie joined the Western Cross Timber area. After further thought, he concluded that the county seat would be located on top of the hill. His calculations and judgment proved correct, when his home and store turned out to be within the limits of Decatur.

The Texas legislature created Wise County in 1856 and named it for Congressman Harry A. Wise of Virginia, who had supported the annexation of Texas to the United States. The legislation creating Wise County specified that an election must be called to select a site for a county seat within five miles of the center of the County and further decreed that the name of the "seat of Justice . . . shall be Taylorsville," in honor of General Zachary Taylor.

Colonel Absalom Bishop was active in the election campaign to have the county seat placed in its present location. The colonel, who was said to have had real estate interests in the area, developed a plan similar to that of McKinney, Texas, for laying out the town.

According to Cliff D. Cates's *Pioneer History*, the contest narrowed down to a struggle between the north and south parts of the county. The vote was so divided ". . . that the choice fell . . . to one of the weaker candidates, with Bishop's hill-top a close second. But . . . certain irregularities were discovered in one of the voting boxes, resulting in its being thrown out, and leaving the choice to fall victoriously into the hands of Bishop. . . ."

On January 7, 1858, Colonel Bishop, then a member of the legislature, had the name of the town changed from Taylorsville to Decatur because, it is said, the colonel did not approve of General Taylor's having been a member of the Whig party.

In 1859, the year in which the initial immigration practically stopped, the Gose family arrived from Sullivan County, Missouri. The family moved south because they sensed the coming of the Civil War. My grandmother, Henrietta Hope Gose, was then five years old.

Between 1860 and 1870 the Civil War and Indian raids caused the population of Wise County to decrease from 3,160 to 1,450. As Federal troops withdrew from the Texas frontier and young men left to be soldiers for the Confederacy, the number of Indian attacks increased. The frontier in the Wise County area receded at a cost of many lives. Some settlers moved eastward to have better protection against raids blamed largely on the Comanches and Kiowas.

Federal troops returned to protect settlers from the Indians after the Civil War and, joined by Texas Rangers, confined the Indians to reservations by 1874. The relative security from Indian raids encouraged immigration, and population surged, as shown by Wise County census figures.

Year of Census	Population
1870	1,450
1880	16,601
1890	24,134
1900	27,116

The pasture land of the Grand Prairie in the eastern part of the county was soon occupied by cattle ranchers, while much of the population increase was in the Western Cross Timbers portion, where small farms were the rule and subsistence farming was practical. The county's population growth was thus largely rural, with most of the newcomers building houses on small tracts of 160 acres, more or less. Early farming methods, especially as applied to the sandy loam of the Cross Timbers region, caused damage that present-day inhabitants are striving to repair. After a few crops, the sandy soil, which probably should never have been plowed, eroded disastrously. Now the land where corn and cotton once thrived is scarred with gullies, some of which are ten feet deep or more. Even so, the Cross Timbers still provides an area of subsistence farming, where families survive on orchards, gardens, small fields, and livestock.

During the era of farm prosperity from 1874 to 1900, Decatur and neighboring communities thrived, and merchants, including saloon keepers, did well. The Butterfield stage route and the Chisholm trail passed through Decatur about 1875, in honor of which the town still sponsors an annual Chisholm trail barbecue and festivities. When the Fort Worth & Denver Railroad built its tracks through the town in 1882, a big crowd gathered to watch the first train pass.

This was the period when an unknown gambler, said to have been a railroad construction worker, shouted "Eighter from Decatur, county seat of Wise" as he rolled the dice when needing an eight to win the pot. The gambler's words somehow caught on. The late Dick Collins, longtime editor of the *Wise County Messenger*, concluded that soldiers from Wise County spread the "Eighter" chant to soldiers from other states during the Spanish-American War and World War I. Proud of its "Eighter from Decatur" notoriety, the town for some fifty years has had signs at its city limits publicizing that saying with a pair of dice showing eight up.

The population of Wise County peaked in 1900. Subsequent censuses reveal the following:

Year of Census	Population
1910	26,450
1920	23,363
1930	19,178
1940	19,074
1950	16,141
1960	17,012
1970	19,687

The recent increase in population must be attributed to the Dallas–Fort Worth metroplex. Decatur, forty miles northwest of Fort Worth, long ago ceased to be a frontier outpost of that city and is now becoming a suburb.

Decatur sits on a hill at the edge of the geographic region called the Grand Prairie and overlooks the post oaks, sand, and loam of the Western Cross Timbers. The Grand Prairie, somewhat like the rich Blackland Prairie to the east, has fertile black soil over limestone, but it is better adapted to ranching than farming. Peanuts, watermelons, fruit, and dairy cattle thrive in the Western Cross Timbers country, where ranches have replaced many of the farms of earlier years in the eroded areas. In some places the black soil of the Grand Prairie has washed over the reddish soil of the Western Cross Timbers. In Decatur's Oaklawn Cemetery some open graves have revealed the soils of both regions.

Decatur and Bridgeport are almost the same size, about 3,500 to 3,700. Other communities in the county are Alvord, Chico, Greenwood, Slidell, Boyd, Aurora, Rhome, Newark, Keeter, Paradise, Cottondale, Boonsville, Balsora, Crafton, and Park Springs.

Many of the dreams of the early settlers have been realized. The distinctive pink granite courthouse with its interior of Vermont marble, built in 1896 at a cost of $110,000, was a cherished improvement that many old-timers saw, enjoyed, and helped pay for. They would be disappointed that Decatur Baptist College, which once claimed to be the oldest junior college in the world, no longer operates. They would be pleased, however, with the facilities of Decatur Independent School District, which has an annual operating budget of over $2 million. Finally, they would be amazed at the wealth produced by the county's oil and gas wells and at the restoration of prairie grass and the correction of erosion in the Cross Timbers National Grassland in the north part of the county.

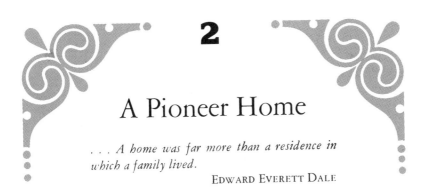

2

A Pioneer Home

. . . A home was far more than a residence in which a family lived.

EDWARD EVERETT DALE

Shortly before school started in September, 1917, Dad hitched our chestnut-colored mare, Fanny, to the buggy before leaving in his secondhand Model T Ford to drive the dusty, bumpy eighty miles to Wichita Falls, where he was starting his career in the oil business. He kissed us goodbye and told us to have a good time visiting Grandpa, Grandma, Uncle Jim, Uncle Bill, Uncle Carl, Uncle David, and Uncle Clarence, who lived on a farm on Sycamore Creek in northeast Wise County.

Mama sat on the right end of the seat, where she could reach the buggy whip. I sat on the left end, and Henry was in the middle. Fanny was a pretty mare and trotted smoothly when the road was level. Otherwise, she pulled strongly uphill and hunched back to keep the buggy from going too fast downhill.

Johnny Dunn waved at us on the square, and we soon crossed the Fort Worth & Denver Railroad track north of town. Within a few miles we passed in front of Mr. Holt's house on the right-hand side of the road. When Mama waved, he nodded his head. He was in a rocking chair and moving slowly back and forth as the warm breeze ruffled his long, gray beard. Henry and I looked at the black patch he wore over the socket where an eye used to be before he lost it in the Civil War.

We were traveling along the edge of the Grand Prairie, where a few yellow blooms were trying vainly to take the place of the multitude of red, white, and pink flowers we had seen there last

April. As we were leaving the Grand Prairie and starting through a stretch of the sandy Cross Timbers, Mama told us, "I've heard that the folks are thinking about selling the farm and moving out west to Haskell County."

Henry and I could not comprehend such a thing, because we had visited the Sycamore Creek farm often. Although I was then seven and Henry almost six, we had already enjoyed many adventures there in spite of, or perhaps because of, our young ages.

To keep us still, Mother began to tell us stories about our grandfather and grandmother. "Your grandfather was fifteen when he traveled with his family in a covered wagon from Crab Orchard, Kentucky, to Texas in 1853. The family stopped in Collin County for a year and then came on to Wise County in 1854. Grandpa enlisted on May 4, 1861, and was a Texas Ranger in a frontier company during the Civil War."

Henry and I interrupted almost in unison: "Oh boy, Grandpa was a Texas Ranger!"

Mama ignored the interruption and concluded her description of Grandpa's military service: "He fought Comanches and Kiowas all along the Red River during the Civil War."

Mama, young and beautiful, appeared even more comely when speaking of her mother. She said: "Your grandmother, Henrietta Hope Gose, was five years old when she traveled in a covered wagon with her family from Sullivan County, Missouri, to Decatur in 1859. She remembers running to Decatur's stockade with the rest of the family when somebody saw Indians near town. And she saw the first train to come to Decatur on the Fort Worth & Denver Railroad."

Henry said, "Mama, I like trains."

"Girls used to marry when they were very young," Mama went on; "Your grandmother was sixteen when she married your grandfather on April 13, 1870. He was twice her age—thirty-two."

I said, "Grandpa sure was old," thinking he had always sported his long, gray beard.

Mama ignored my remark and continued: "Your grandpa had a

good farm with a nice house just a few miles south of Decatur. Most of my brothers and sisters were born on that farm; Eureka, Sammie, Mamie, Ollie, Stephen, Jim, Bill, and Carl were all born there. Then your grandfather moved the family to Indian Territory near Ardmore."

Henry asked why.

Looking disturbed, Mama said, "Because your grandpa gave up that good farm."

I asked, "Why?"

Mama frowned and replied: "Well, your grandpa wanted to make some money, so he went into the furniture business with a preacher. He lost the business and the farm too."

Henry inquired again, "Why?"

Mama answered, "Because he let the preacher run the store."

"Oh!"

Mama continued, and I thought her eyes watered just a little as she confessed, "And so I was born in Indian Territory in 1890."

Henry asked, "Did Grandpa have a farm in Indian Territory?"

Mama replied, "No, he farmed for the Indians."

"When did the family come back to Wise County?" I asked.

Mama's face brightened a bit as she announced: "Well, Irene and David were born in Indian Territory, too; then we moved back in covered wagons in 1896. The boys rode horses and herded the livestock along with the wagons, and we moved into the house on Sycamore Creek where we are going right now. Your Uncle Clarence was born in that house in 1898."

The road was level, and Fanny was trotting smoothly. We noticed the Pickett home on the left side of the road, and Mama remarked that Mr. Pickett had once set a world record in calf roping at Chicago. Henry and I were squirming, but Mama ignored our activity until I started poking him in the ribs and pinching him. She slapped me lightly on the cheek and sat between us just as Henry was starting to swing a roundhouse right at my middle.

A few turns of the road before Grandpa's house came into view, Mama said firmly: "My father and mother are pioneers; I want you to remember that. Your grandpa has been a farmer all his life except when he was a Texas Ranger. Farmers and ranchers are the ones who worked hard and raised families and are the ones who really settled the West—not the gun shooters you hear about."

Mama continued, "Your grandpa and grandma are living in a pioneer house; I want you to look at everything and remember what a pioneer house is like."

Impressed with her gravity, Henry and I answered somewhat simultaneously, "We'll look at everything, Mama, but we don't want them to move to Haskell County."

We rounded the last turn in the road just before noon and saw Uncle Clarence washing his face in a pan on a shelf at the corner of the house. He was lucky because he was nineteen and had not been drafted for World War I. He met us at the gate and grinned: "How are you, Pearl; hello, boys. Pearl, you and the boys get out and go in for dinner while I unhitch Fanny and give her some water and oats in the horse lot."

Mama had a way of appearing to glide out of a buggy without visible effort. While Mama made her graceful exit, Henry and I jumped out, ran toward the gate, and stopped to look at the house with special interest because of Mama's admonition. The house faced us, since we were on the south side. The front porch was about eight feet wide and extended from the windows of the guest room to the windows of the dining room, which was not very far. The top of the roof was straight and parallel to the porch. A chimney was at the east end. Each window had four panes of glass in the bottom half and four in the upper half. The house looked as though it had been painted some time in the past. Our minds were young and fresh and grasped the appearance of the familiar house quickly, but we did not discuss or think much about the details until years later.

Just then Grandma, wearing a dark-figured calico dress and white apron, came out of the front door and greeted us affectionately, saying, "You're just in time for dinner," meaning the big noon meal. Grandma held the screen door open as we went into the entrance hall and turned through the door on the left. A curtain closed off all but the front end of the entrance hall.

Mama put her suitcase down in the dining room, and we sat at a long table with Grandma at the north end next to the kitchen and Grandpa facing her from the south end. We sat with our uncles along the sides of the table. Without further ado, Grandpa asked a short blessing and passed the fried chicken.

While the big platter was moving toward me, I looked hungrily around and saw hominy, cream gravy, biscuits, molasses, honey, mashed potato salad, green beans, turnip greens, and a big cake in the middle of the table. Everybody had large glasses of water except Henry and me, and we had milk. All ten of us ate heartily, but we still didn't eat all the food; there always seemed to be more.

No fried chicken can be better than Grandma's. Her chicken was fresh, the birds having chased grasshoppers and eaten corn the very morning of the dinner. Grandma separated the pieces neatly at the joints, not like the pieces hacked apart with a meat cleaver at today's restaurants. Her chicken, fried in an iron skillet to a delicate brown in home-rendered lard, was crisp and tasty.

After Henry and I finally finished generous helpings of yellow cake with caramel icing, we remembered Mama's plea to pay attention to what a pioneer home is like. We looked around the dining room, and the first thing that caught our attention was Grandpa and Grandma's double bed in the northeast corner of the room. The bed was neatly made up with a pretty wedding ring quilt on top and fluffy pillows at the north end. We turned toward the window and saw a Singer sewing machine with a chair placed where the light was good. For some reason, Henry looked at the ceiling, where he saw a wood frame, somewhat bigger than a quilt, suspended a few inches below the ceiling. He asked Grandma what it was.

"That's a quilt frame, Henry Will. Sometimes a few of my friends come here, and we let the frame down so we can sit around it and work together on a quilt. Some people call that a quilting party."

"I'd like to go to a quilting party," Henry told her.

In the meantime, I was daydreaming out the window. I saw a

little hopping spider capture a fly on the outside of the screen, and then I noticed a stick holding the window open. I asked, "Uncle Carl, what's a stick doing in the window?"

"I'll declare, I've never seen such curious rascals. That stick is holding the window up. Our windows don't have counterbalancing weights like you have at home. If you boys have to know everything about this place, I'll go over it with you when I get back from plowing."

That seemed like a good idea; "Yes sir, we want to look around."

Then I noticed a little table with a coal oil lamp on top and a shelf near the floor, where magazines and books were stacked. I also saw a dresser near the south end of the bed and some pretty watercolors on the wall. Later I learned that Aunt Irene and Mama had painted them.

After dinner, Mama picked up her little suitcase, and we followed her into the hall and through a door on the other side into the combination parlor and guest room on the east end of the house, where we were to stay. A fireplace, the only one in the house, was at the end of the room. A handsome clock on the mantle showed the time, the day of the week, and the day of the month. The room was furnished with a double bed, a small table bearing a washbasin and pitcher, a tall walnut wardrobe (which took the place of a closet), a mirror, three or four chairs, and a hooked rug. A large picture of Uncle Sammie, the son who was killed riding a runaway horse that swerved under the low branch of a tree, hung on the north wall over the bed.

Mama unpacked a few things and said, "Boys, I'll show you where the girls used to sleep." She led us through a door on the north side into a smaller room built shedlike against the back of the house. Its two doors opened into the parlor–guest room and the hall. The room was crowded with three beds, a mirror, and a chest of drawers. There was no provision for heat, and Mama remembered, "One winter it was so cold that the coal oil got too thick to run up the wick of the lamp, so we had to go to bed in the dark." Then, while Mama went to the kitchen to help Grandma with the dishes,

Henry and I went outside and ran around back of the house toward the creek.

At the creek, which was about a hundred yards from the house, we waded, threw rocks, and looked up in the big trees, hoping to see squirrels, but we got only occasional glimpses as they ran around to the opposite sides of the trees.

Finally, we ran up a big gully toward the house. Near the end of the gully, where the ground rose sharply, Henry yelled, "This is where Grandma killed the snake that almost got us!" The grass was dry, and we ran up and down the sides of the gully.

In the preceding spring, when the grass was soft and moist, we had been playing there when we saw a snake. Frightened, we tried to run out of the gully but kept slipping back toward the snake on the moist grass. We started yelling as we tried to get out, too scared to run away from the house toward the creek. Grandma heard us, came running with a hoe, and dispatched the snake with one or two quick chops. Memory of the snake made it more fun to run up and down the banks. Finally, we trudged toward the house and saw our uncles coming home from the field.

While we were waiting for the men to wash their hands and faces and comb their hair, we saw Grandpa sitting on the porch with the right leg of his trousers rolled up to his knee. He was putting salve on a bad-looking sore on his shin, and we moved closer to see the sore more clearly. I asked, "Grandpa, what's that?"

"Well, one day I slipped and cut my shin on a disc plow, and I don't think it ever will get well." From what I heard later, it never did.

Uncle Carl was about to go in the front door when Henry and I yelled, "Uncle Carl, you promised to show us around."

He smiled and said, "Well, you rascals have seen everything in the house."

"No," I argued, "we don't know what's behind that curtain back of the front door."

He pulled the curtain back, exposing a row of beds, and said: "This was an old house when Pa bought it, and this hall was an open dog run. We called it that because it was a long, straight hall that ran from front to back of the house and was open at both ends, so a dog could run straight through. Pa closed it in so we boys would have a place to sleep, and your grandmother put this curtain up so we could have some privacy." We saw a little chest of drawers with a bowl and pitcher on it, a mirror, and a razor strap hanging on the wall. We nodded our heads solemnly, and Uncle Carl said, "Come on, and I'll show you around."

We started in the front yard where a grindstone, mounted on a homemade wood frame, was under a cedar tree. Uncle Carl said, "One of us boys turned the handle while Pa sharpened tools, and I'd bet I have turned that grindstone over five hundred miles."

I gave the grindstone a few turns while Henry was looking back at the house. A prospective craftsman even at age six, he asked, "Uncle Carl, how is the house built?"

That was a more involved question than Henry realized. Uncle Carl looked back at the house and answered: "Well, that's not a frame house like yours; it's a box house. That means the outside wall isn't separated from the inside wall by two-by-fours. The inside wall is made with shiplap lumber that runs parallel to the ground, and the outside wall is made of one-by-twelves vertical to the ground. The inside wall is nailed directly to the outside wall, and the cracks between the one-by-twelves are covered with narrow strips of wood. That's called board-and-bat siding."

Uncle Carl's technical explanation was longer than our span of interest, and we spent most of the time looking at a bird nest. Strangely, though, his words entered our memories, and years later we understood how a box house was built.

We walked around the west end of the house, where we looked at the garden, which, except for turnips, was almost bare after a dry summer. Nearby we saw a hopper-shaped wood rack with a tray beneath it, and Henry asked, "What's that, Uncle Carl?"

The rack was half full of ashes; Uncle Carl explained, "We drip water through the ashes to make lye."

An earlier experience made me wary of lye, and I asked, "What do you want that for?" Uncle Carl explained that Grandma used the lye to make hominy from corn and soap from lard.

Henry looked left toward the creek and said, "There's a big old black washpot."

"Yes," Uncle Carl told us, "that's a twenty-gallon pot, and it's more than two feet across the top. We need a big one for our family."

We walked toward the pot; its three stubby legs were set on bricks to make the pot high enough for a blazing fire underneath. Grandma boiled the clothes in the pot and scrubbed them on a washboard. Clothes had a pleasant, fresh odor after Grandma washed them and dried them in the sun.

Two "ears" or little handles, on opposite sides near the top of the pot, were used to move it.

We looked back to our right at the north side of the smokehouse and saw a rack about two feet high built on the side of the little building. Three washtubs and a washboard hung above the rack, and a bottle of bluing was sitting on the end.

Uncle Carl continued, "Yes, we wash clothes in the washpot, but we also use it when we make soap or hominy and when we render lard at hog-killing time."

Uncle Carl opened the door to the smokehouse, and we saw home-cured hams and sides of bacon hanging from the joists. Henry's sharp eyes discovered a shotgun-shell box stored safely in a corner. When Henry lifted the top, we saw Uncle Clarence's collection of arrowheads, most of which he had found in freshly plowed fields after rains.

We recognized the two-holer outhouse downhill from the smokehouse to the northeast. Uncle Carl's only comment was, "That's for the womenfolk except in emergency. The men use the horse lot, but you boys can use either one." We thought it good to have an option.

We walked on east of the house where Uncle Carl pointed to

several square boxes under the trees and inquired if we knew what they were. We announced in unison, "Bee hives," having had a painful experience there earlier.

The pigpen was about fifty feet ahead of us, and the pigs were noisy because they thought we might be bringing them a big bucket of kitchen scraps, called slop.

We went east about thirty more yards to the barn and horse lot and climbed over the high board fence. Uncle Carl showed us the hay and corn in the barn, drew some water from the twenty-foot well, and poured it in a wood trough that extended through the fence so livestock on both sides could drink. When we thought to do so, we were careful to look where we stepped. As we were leaving, we noticed the chickens beginning to go to roost in the chicken house in a corner of the horse lot.

As we started walking back toward the house, Uncle Carl pointed out the turkey roost to our right toward the creek and explained that turkeys would scatter out among the trees along the creek if they didn't have a special place to roost. This roost was built with four vertical poles supporting a framework along which a number of other poles were laid parallel to each other. Uncle Carl said: "One time a big old hoot owl decided he liked the turkey roost and started staying there at night. The turkeys were scared and wouldn't use the roost, even though the old owl didn't seem interested in catching any of them."

As we walked toward the house again, we passed the orchard, where trees produced apples, peaches, plums, and pears.

We stopped at the well near the southeast corner of the house, and while Uncle Carl was drawing a bucket of water he told us, "This well is thirty feet deep and walled with rock."

He handed me the yellow gourd dipper half full of water. I drank some of it and started to put the dipper and remaining water back in the bucket. Uncle Carl stopped me; "No, we all drink out of the same dipper, but we don't put water back in the bucket after taking a sip. Just pour it on these flowers by the well." Henry then had a drink and did not need instructions about what to do with unused water.

The well's rope went over a pulley that hung over the well from a horizontal piece of wood, which was supported by two vertical two-by-fours that extended up along the sides of the well. The rock wall in the well rose about three and a half feet above the ground, and the top was covered with boards that had a hinged door in the middle. "Look here," Uncle Carl said, "as I draw the water out of the well, I loop the rope around the stick that comes out from the right-hand vertical two-by-four."

When he finished drinking, Uncle Carl lowered the bucket a foot or two below the hinged door and left it in place by making a tight loop around the stick where the rest of the rope was looped. Then he closed the door on top of the well.

Our attention strayed, as it had when Uncle Carl had explained the construction of a box house, but his description and instructions returned to us in later years.

Uncle Carl took us to the shelf at the corner of the house, where the men washed after work, but we were too short to reach it. He poured a pan of water for us and handed us a cube of brown home-made soap. We set the pan on the grass and did a fair job of washing our hands. The soap did not make much lather but did a good job of loosening the dirt. When Uncle Carl put the pan back on the shelf, we noticed a little mirror hanging on the wall and saw a comb and brush on the shelf.

We went into the dining-sewing-bedroom, where Grandma patted us on the heads and said, "Boys, supper is almost ready." We knew supper wouldn't be a big meal like dinner, but we also knew there would be plenty.

Grandpa, the uncles, Mama, Henry, and I sat around the table and talked as we crumbled homemade bread into our glasses of milk and ate cornbread, fried chicken left from dinner, molasses, preserves, fresh butter, and cake. There was neither a blessing at the beginning nor a formal ending. The light supper was a relaxed come-and-go affair.

Uncle Jim related funny stories about what had happened in town on "first Monday" (the town's monthly trade day), when he bought a mule from Ben Green. Uncle Bill didn't talk much, but he did tell us about an article he had read in a magazine named *Physical Culture*. Uncle David, our handsome uncle who used crutches because he had been crippled by polio when he was a boy, said his grip was strong enough to pick up a cane-bottom chair by the bottom front rung and lift it off the floor with one hand straight up without tilting the chair. Uncle Clarence challenged him to prove it, and Uncle David did.

Grandma, in accordance with her custom, didn't eat supper but listened and took part in the conversation while making sure everybody else had plenty to eat. Supper must not be necessary for good health; she lived to be almost ninety-eight.

After supper, the men gathered around the coal oil lamps on the table and read newspapers, magazines, and books. Mama helped Grandma in the kitchen before crocheting on a piece for our dresser. Grandpa got up and started a little fire in the parlor fireplace in honor of our visit. When Grandma came out of the kitchen and asked Uncle Jim to bring in a washtub and two buckets of water, I knew Henry and I were in for trouble.

She heated the water on the kitchen stove and soon called Henry and me into the kitchen, where she asked us to remove our clothes and stand in the tub. With understandable reluctance, we followed her instructions. We acted embarrassed when she began scrubbing us with a washrag and plenty of soap. Grandma said, "It's all right; I won't look at you," and she completed a thorough scrubbing while looking to the side. Having raised seven sons, she had no problem completing the chore.

We put on pajamas and went to the parlor–guest room but were not sleepy after the bath. We started playing with the fire in the fireplace. We got a few live coals out on the hearth and rolled them around with the poker.

In the meantime, Grandpa, with his extensive experience raising boys, did not hear us playing and knew we were either asleep or in trouble. When he walked through the door and saw what we were doing, he stood as straight as he must have stood in the Texas Ranger company. He said only, "Boys!" But his eyes blazed almost as brightly as the coals. With his long, white beard, he looked like a picture we had seen of Moses when he caught the children of Israel worshiping the golden calf. We quickly understood his point of view, pushed the coals back in the fire, and went to bed. We didn't play with live coals there anymore.

I got out of bed early in the morning, awakened by the sound of the coffee grinder and the aroma of home-cured bacon. The kitchen, like the girl's room, was built shedlike on the north side of the house and had a door opening near the dining room table. Although the sun was barely showing in the east, Grandma was cooking breakfast later than usual because she didn't want to disturb her guests. I stood at the door and watched her make biscuits. She pulled the flour bin open and left it that way while she put in shortening, baking powder, and whatever else she used. She moved quickly and didn't measure anything. When all the ingredients were in the bin, she kneaded the material until it picked up just the right amount of flour. Then she lifted the dough from the bin and rolled it out on a floured breadboard with her rolling pin. She greased the bottom of a large pan, cut the biscuits out of the dough with the top of a baking powder can, laid them in the pan, and put the pan in the oven, which was next to the firebox of the stove. I could hardly wait for Grandma to take her biscuits out. When she finally took the pan out, the biscuits were a beautiful chestnut brown that reminded me of our pretty mare, Fanny.

Soon the fragrance of home-ground coffee blended with that of bacon, and the family gathered at the table for breakfast, a meal only slightly more formal than supper. We had biscuits, scrambled eggs, bacon, redeye gravy, fresh butter, and wild plum jelly. Henry and I had milk, while the grownups had coffee.

After breakfast, Henry and I went into the kitchen together to see what was in it. We noticed a door opening to the yard on the west side, saw a large bucket for kitchen scraps used to slop the hogs, and inspected the black, wood-burning kitchen stove. We saw a worktable, a chest that had a flour bin, the utensils hanging on the wall, shelves for staples and canned food, the coffee grinder, a can of coal oil with a potato stuck on the spout, and the evaporative cooler covered with a wet sheet that extended into a water trough at the bottom.

Grandpa and the uncles left for the fields, saying they thought they would be through plowing by noon. Because they were gone, Henry and I felt that it wasn't necessary to prove our manhood by going to the horse lot but went to the outhouse instead, fully occupying the two-holer. Henry got the mail-order catalogue first and looked at it, while I pondered the shiny, black spiders in the irregular webs in the upper corners. The spiders had red hourglass markings and didn't seem aggressive. (Years later we realized that the friendly spiders were black widows.) Before leaving, we used a piece of shingle to take ashes from a bucket and scatter the ashes through the holes for sanitation.

Henry and I then walked to Uncle Steve Perrin's house, which was about half a mile to the south and a little east. We wanted to play with our cousins, Julian and John Paul. Grandpa's big dog Blackie went part of the way with us as we walked along a path through dew-covered grass that glistened in the morning sun.

When we got there, Aunt Julia greeted us with, "I just want you boys to see Julian," and we were alarmed at the tone of her voice. When Julian came out, we saw that his left eye was swollen shut, and his face was puffed up. He said a bumblebee had stung him near the eye. When John Paul came out, he pointed to Julian and smiled widely, but he didn't laugh. He knew that though Julian couldn't see very well nothing was wrong with his hearing.

We went west of the house, where some mustang grapevines grew over a small clump of post oak trees. We swung on some of the vines that dangled from the trees. Later we climbed a vine into a tree, where we found a network of vines that connected several trees. Julian was very careful during all this activity, because he saw poorly with one eye and not at all with the other.

After we quit playing in the vines, we looked west on the road and saw Uncle Steve going by in his new Maxwell car. Uncle Steve had gained considerable prestige in the Sycamore community when he bought the Maxwell, but the prestige had a price, because the car did not not seem to run very long at a time.

Soon it was almost noon, and Aunt Julia invited us to eat with her family. Henry and I decided, however, to go back to Grandma's because we had not asked permission to stay all day. Julian managed a moderately cheerful goodbye in spite of his condition.

As we walked back, the grass no longer had a fairyland appearance; the dew had long since evaporated. Instead, the grass just looked its usual dry-summer brown.

Grandpa was lying on his back on a cot on the front porch and holding a flyswatter, with which his aim was deadly.

Our uncles came from the field a bit later than usual and told us they had finished the plowing. After they washed and combed their hair, we went into the dining room, where Grandma had dinner on the table. The main item was fried home-cured ham, supplemented with sweet potatoes, homemade light bread, fresh butter, beets, turnips, buttermilk, and pie made from green mustang grapes Grandma had canned earlier in the summer. After Grandpa's usual short blessing, we ate until we were full.

After dinner, Uncle Bill suggested, "Let's take a bath." The other uncles approved as they got up from the table. Henry and I, having survived Grandma's scrubbing the night before, were interested in how the uncles proposed to take baths. They got towels and clean clothes, went out the front door, and turned eastward toward the barn. Henry and I followed as they walked past the barn and about half a mile east of the house, where water from a spring flowed through a wood trough. One after the other, they sat in the trough, lathered themselves with Grandma's homemade soap, and dried themselves with big towels. When they were through, Henry asked, "How do you take baths when it's cold?"

Uncle Jim answered with a chuckle, "Why, at home we bathe in a washtub like everybody else."

After we returned to the house, the uncles started doing various chores. Uncle Jim repaired a gate at the horse lot; Uncle Carl took the ashes out of the stove and the fireplace and put them in the hopper back of the house; Uncle Bill packed his clothes for a trip to Fort Worth to look for a job; Uncle David reset the big clock on the mantle in the guest room, which had run down and lost its synchronization of striking and showing the time, the day of the week, and the day of the month; and Uncle Clarence chopped wood for the kitchen stove. In the meantime, Grandpa took a nap on the cot on the front porch, stretched out on his back as usual.

Henry and I went to the kitchen to get sugar cookies, which Grandma kept in a dishpan covered with a dish towel. The cookies were always good, and the pan seldom empty.

Grandma, still in the kitchen, patiently plunged the dasher up and down in the big crockery churn. Henry and I offered our services and gained experience in making butter and buttermilk. We watched Grandma gather the butter out of the churn, work it with a little wood paddle, and press it into a round wood mold. When Grandma pushed the butter out of the form with a plunger that extended through a hole in the top of the mold, we saw a beautiful pound of yellow butter with the imprint of a flower on top.

When she finished with the butter, Grandma said, "Now, boys, I'm going to doctor the baby chicks."

We asked, "Are the baby chicks sick?"

"No, they aren't really sick, but they have mites."

"What's mites?" Henry wanted to know.

"They're tiny bugs that like to eat on baby chicks. Come on, I'll show you."

Grandma got a cardboard box, took the chicks from a belligerent old mother hen, and put them in the box. She then took the chicks out one by one, dusted them with a strong-smelling brown powder, and released them to the mother hen, who was less interested than when Grandma was picking the chicks up.

I asked, "Grandma, what's that funny-smelling powder?"

"It's snuff."

Henry inquired, "Grandma, who uses the snuff?"

Grandma looked slightly sick at her stomach when she answered,

"Henry Will Barton, nobody at this house uses snuff. The only thing it is good for is killing bugs."

We followed Grandma to the chicken house after she doctored the baby chicks, and we watched her gather eggs from straw nests and from various other nests the hens had improvised in the barn. Grandma held up the bottom of her apron with her left hand while she put the eggs in it with her right hand.

By that time, Uncle Clarence had slopped the hogs and fed the chickens. He was beginning to milk the cows when he turned to me and asked, "Jim Tom, do you want to milk Old Bossy?"

I said sure and squeezed a teat, but nothing came out; the milk seemed to run back into her bag. I tried again, with the same result.

Uncle Clarence laughed: "You'll never get any milk that way. First, squeeze the teat with your forefinger and then squeeze with the other three fingers to make it come out." I tried again with minimum success. Old Bossy, who obviously did not approve of the proceedings, turned her head, looked at me, and popped me a good one in the face with her tail, a more muscular appendage than I had thought. At that point Uncle Clarence took over and said, "I'd better milk Old Bossy before she kicks you."

When we walked back to the house, we found Grandpa sitting on the steps, picking his teeth with a sharpened peach tree twig. (Maybe there is something good for teeth in peach tree sap, because he had all his teeth in good working order when he died two years later at eighty-one.)

Henry asked, "Grandpa, why do you have that long beard?"

Grandpa answered, scarcely noticing us, "To keep my neck warm."

After a good supper that evening and a savory breakfast the next morning, we rode back to Decatur in the buggy with Mama. This time she sat between us the whole ten miles. We weren't restless on the trip back, having had plenty of exercise and many experiences to tell Mama.

A few weeks later we learned that Grandpa (then seventy-nine), Uncle Jim, Uncle Carl, and Uncle Stephen had bought farmland to the west, in Haskell County, and were planning to move in January, 1918.

We also heard that the Perrins were going to have a hog killing on the first cold day so they would have plenty of meat when starting a new life.

Dad was home when hog-killing weather came in late November, and he drove us to the farm in his Model T Ford.

The day was cold and clear. The uncles killed three hogs, bled the hogs by cutting the jugulars, scalded and scraped the carcasses, and hung the hogs by the hind legs from limbs of the trees east of the house. Then they gutted the hogs, saved the livers to be eaten soon, and carefully removed the fat from the viscera for later rendering. The uncles cut the carcasses into hams, pork loins, sides of bacon, roasts, and sausage meat. They then put the meat on the low roof of the front porch to chill overnight. The next morning they started the curing processes and later stored the meat in the smokehouse, to be taken to Haskell County in the move.

A few months later, Mama described the move to us. The livestock, farm machinery, and furniture were loaded on two freight cars of the Fort Worth & Denver at Decatur. Uncle Jim rode on the freight train to take care of the family property. At Wichita Falls the two cars were switched to the Wichita Valley Railroad, a short line that ran to Haskell. On this second stage of the trip the engineer told Uncle Jim the two cars were going to be switched off at a country siding. Naturally, Uncle Jim got excited and told the engineer the Wichita Valley would have to feed the livestock and pay damages. Finally, the engineer grinned and told Uncle Jim he was just kidding. Uncle Jim, a practical joker himself, eventually got a laugh out of the hoax.

In the meantime, the rest of the family bounced slowly over the 160 miles in the Maxwell and two Model T Fords. Travel in open touring cars in January was cold.

Farming prospects were not favorable when the family arrived, 1917 having been the driest year on record in Texas. The next year, 1918, was one of average rainfall, however, and the family harvested fairly good crops.

In the summer of 1918 Mama, Henry, and I spent two or three weeks with Grandpa and Grandma. Their Haskell County house was more of a farm structure than a pioneer house; it had a screened sleeping porch with a cistern in it.

A large prairie dog town was across the road from the mailbox about a quarter of a mile east of the house. Henry and I watched these little animals standing on the mounds at the entrances to their tunnels and saw them dive in when alarmed. Once we saw two coyotes between the house and the mailbox. The crawfishing was unbelievable by Wise County standards. Julian and John Paul went crawfishing with us at the tank on Lake Creek about seventy-five yards behind Grandpa's barn and caught a bucketful. Having nothing better to do with the unfortunate critters, we fed them to the chickens.

Rainfall the following year, 1919, was one of the heaviest on record. That was the year Julian and John Paul caught prairie dogs by drowning them out of their deep holes when water was standing on the prairie. The boys cut ditches through the dikelike mounds the animals built around the openings to their holes. In June of that year, the Steve Perrin family visited Wise County, and Julian and John Paul gave Henry and me a young prairie dog, which promptly escaped by digging a tunnel under the side of the box we placed over him.

Later that summer we visited the Perrin family again and learned to swim in the tank with Grandpa and the uncles. We didn't have bathing suits, and the women didn't come near the tank when we were swimming.

That was the summer Grandpa bought a pair of wild mules, which were delivered to the horse lot with their front legs hobbled. Our big, strong uncles were understandably reluctant to remove the hobbles because the risk was great. Grandpa gave his sons a sort of contemptuous look, climbed over the fence, got down on his knees by the front legs of the mules, and calmly removed the hobbles.

Late in August, 1919, we received word that Grandpa was very sick, and Dad drove us to Haskell County in his new Model T Ford.

The morning after we arrived, the bedoom was crowded; Grandma, her sons and daughters, a few sons-in-law, and a few grandchildren stood quietly in the room. I stood by Uncle Carl, just a few feet back from the bed. I looked at Grandpa, who was lying on his back, which was the way he usually slept, but this time was different. Someone whispered that Grandpa was dying. Dr. Gentry, a son-in-law, was there looking as puzzled and sorrowful as the rest of us. Grandpa was dying in Haskell County, the most recent stop in his westward trek, which had begun at Crab Orchard, Kentucky, in 1853, when he was fifteen. Now it was September 1, 1919.

I looked at Grandpa's beard, which was white and neatly combed as usual. I looked at his eyes, and he seemed to be sleeping. How could Grandpa be so still? He was a man of action, having fought the Comanches and Kiowas as a Texas Ranger.

I looked at Grandpa's face, often ruddy from his work in the fields. His skin was as white as the paint on the wrought-iron bedstead. He did not look like a man who had farmed for the Indians after fighting them.

I looked at the sheet that covered Grandpa's body and revealed an athletic figure. Uncle Clarence told me that only two weeks ago Grandpa had ridden a horse bareback, hitting it with a cornstalk to make it run faster.

I looked at Uncle Carl, who had cared for Grandpa during the past week of illness. Uncle Carl stepped to the side of the bed, placed his hand over Grandpa's heart for a while, stepped back, and said, "He's gone."

I looked at Grandpa's face and saw a tear in the corner of his eye.

I heard some subdued sobbing as those in the room walked slowly toward the other three rooms of the house.

The family, being practical, did not take Grandpa's body to Wise County for burial on the lot with his son Sammie, who had been killed by the runaway horse in 1900. Instead, burial was in the Haskell cemetery, where cedars grow in the grave area and native mesquites flourish outside the fence.

After Grandpa's death, Uncle Carl and Uncle Jim operated the farm ten years. Then Uncle Carl moved westward to Deaf Smith County in 1929 and bought land on the High Plains near the New Mexico border. In 1936 Uncle Jim left Haskell County and joined Carl in wheat and cattle farming and ranching, and Grandma moved to the town of Haskell to live with Aunt Irene Ballard, Aunt Ollie Freeman, and Uncle David in Irene's house. Grandma died in Haskell in 1952, a few months before her ninety-eighth birthday.

In the meantime, Uncles Carl and Jim survived the depression and the dust bowl, while acquiring a sizeable wheat and cattle ranch and a section of irrigated land. Grandpa had left Kentucky in 1853 to find prosperity; his sons found it a hundred years later.

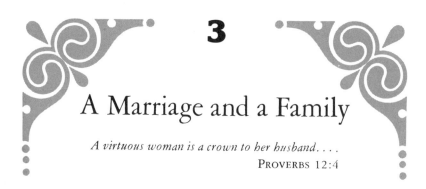

3

A Marriage and a Family

A virtuous woman is a crown to her husband....
PROVERBS 12:4

When Dad and Mama married on Saturday, June 5, 1909, she was about seven weeks short of her nineteenth birthday, and he was almost thirty-three. All arrangements for the ceremony were obviously made by a man, namely, Dad. A wedding like theirs had probably never taken place in Wise County or anywhere else.

The *Wise County Messenger* carried the story of the wedding the following week on Friday, June 11, 1909. The editor, relying on his general knowledge of the Perrin family, did not verify the facts, with the result that his account, quoted below, was inaccurate as to the place of residence of the family and also the location of the wedding. Furthermore, the story was misleading as to the hour the wedding occurred. The newspaper account was as follows:

> Miss Pearl Perrin and Mr. Henry W. Barton were united in marriage last Saturday morning at the home of the bride's parents in the Sycamore community, Rev. S. C. Riddle, pastor of the local M.E. church performing the ceremony. The bride is one of our county's fairest girls, charming, cultured and refined and a member of one of the best and most prominent families in this section. The groom, Henry Barton, is well known to our people as a prince of good fellows, a scholar and a gentleman, and is worthy of the love and esteem of the splendid girl he has won. After a brief visit to Mr. Barton's old home in Tennessee, they will return and reside in Decatur, where he will again take up the duties of superintendent of our local public school.

The Perrin residence at that time was not in the Sycamore community, where the family had lived for years. They were then living on a farm called Consuelo near the north limits of Decatur. The farm was owned by Uncle John G. Gose, and the Perrins lived there several years to help their children go to high school.

Furthermore, the wedding was not in the bride's home but was at the preacher's parsonage, with the preacher's wife being the only witness, and it took place shortly before 6:00 A.M., an ungodly hour for such an event.

Dad must have picked Mama up in his buggy about 5:00 A.M. They rode to the parsonage, Dad having previously urged the Reverend S. C. Riddle to conduct a short ceremony.

Dad, upset by the length of the service, said many times later, "That preacher used the longest service in the book." The procedure must have seemed longer than it really was.

The ostensible reason for the unusual timing of the wedding was that the Forth Worth & Denver passenger train no. 6 stopped briefly at Decatur at 6:30 A.M. Uncles Carl and David went to the depot in a buggy to get Dad's horse and buggy and take them back to the farm. When they got to the depot, they had a fleeting glimpse of their beautiful sister through a car window as the train made its jerky start toward Fort Worth.

The subject was not discussed by the family in later years, but Dad could have arranged to leave on trains that went through Decatur later in the day. Passenger trains no. 2 and no. 4 departed at 2:50 P.M. and 4:35 P.M. respectively.

The honeymooners went to Galveston, where they stayed at the Galvez Hotel and met other newlyweds. They did not go into the surf, Galveston's main attraction. They did not have swimming suits, and Dad did not want other men looking at Mama's shapely figure, anyway.

They left Galveston and made the long train trip to Tennessee to visit Dad's family. On arriving at Shelbyville, Dad picked up Mama's suitcase in the presence of some of the relatives. The suitcase snapped open, spilling Mama's pretty undergarments and dresses. The incident made such an impression on the eighteen-year-old girl that she was concerned with suitcase locks and straps the rest of her life. Once in later years she even tied a little rope around her suitcase to keep from being embarrassed that way again.

During the honeymoon visit to Tennessee, Dad's brother-in-law Samuel P. Davis died, leaving a widow and five children virtually without support. Dad, being the oldest son, felt a tribal loyalty to his family. Grandmother Barton, Aunt Sallie (the widow), and the five children soon moved to Red Oak, Texas, and Dad furnished financial support for years.

How did a thirty-three-year-old man from Tennessee happen to marry a beautiful daughter of pioneer parents in Decatur, Texas? He was the high school principal when she was valedictorian of the class of 1908. He was authoritarian, and she was just a girl.

The courtship started after Mama's graduation. She got a teacher's certificate by passing an examination given locally and was employed as a teacher at Slidell, a community ten or twelve miles from Decatur, near the family home where she had been raised. At Slidell she lived in a little house with the other teacher, Miss Austin, who had been Mama's teacher at nearby Sycamore a few years earlier.

Dad's letters to "Miss Perrin" were both formal and loving, and she wrote "Mr. Barton" letters that he considered encouraging. He was also dutiful about riding to Slidell in his buggy for visits.

On Monday, March 8, 1909, Dad wrote Mama on a postcard bearing a photograph of the faculty of Decatur public school. The seven women teachers, "old maids," wore white shirtwaist blouses with high collars and long, dark skirts. Their dresses and their hairstyles conformed to the Gibson Girl fashion in vogue at that time. Dad and the principal wore dark suits, white shirts, stiff collars, and black bow ties.

Dad's message was about his trip to Slidell on Sunday, the preceding day:

Monday afternoon, Mar. 8, '09.
How has school been today, Miss Perrin? It has been quite good with me for Monday.
I reached home last night at ten, and My! what a fine night's sleep

I did have. Mr. Balthrop came back with me, so I did not go to sleep in my buggy.

Don't you think this is a handsome set [meaning the photograph of the faculty]?

Best wishes

Henry

Say yes

Later that month on March 25, the *Decatur News* published a headline saying, "Cyclone at Greenwood and Slidell—Nine Killed." Eight of those killed were in the Rice family.

The little house where Mama and Miss Austin lived was blown off its foundation. In the freakish way of tornadoes, the kerosene lamp landed upright and unbroken on the floor and continued to burn, and the dishes fell on the floor without breaking.

Dad, hearing of the tornado early in the day, may have set a horse-and-buggy record driving to Slidell and arrived before any of Mama's family did. The storm damaged the little school building badly and therefore marked the end of the spring school term. Dad helped Mama get her things together and took her home to her family.

Dad's quick reaction to Mama's desperate situation was probably the turning point in his successful courtship. It is difficult, however, to believe that any member of the class of 1908 could have competed successfully for Mama's affection against a rival as formidable and determined as Dad.

After the honeymoon, Dad rented a little house next to Aunt Lizzie Renshaw's place, about three blocks west of the courthouse square, and I was born there almost fourteen months after the wedding. There was agreement that I should be named for my grandfathers, James Perrin and John Thomas Barton. Someone said, "Well, James Thomas is a pretty name."

Dad, a man of strong convictions, replied, "No; I'm going to name him Jim Tom, and I'm going to call him Jim Tom," and there was no further discussion.

[33]

My brother, Henry Will, was born almost eighteen months later, probably in the little four-room (not counting kitchen or bathroom) house Dad built two blocks south of the school building. Dad's name was Henry Wilburn. He wanted the new baby to be named for him but abhorred the idea of having a "Junior" in the family. Dad solved the problem by naming the baby Henry Will.

During the early years of their marriage, Dad was something of a father figure to my mother as well as a husband. He bought Mama a piano and arranged for piano and voice lessons. He encouraged her in art, and she responded by painting pictures that are still on display. When she had two little boys, however, Mama gave up painting but continued the piano and voice lessons for several years. Through it all, Mama addressed Dad as Mr. Barton and continued to do so for some twenty-seven years, after which she managed to change to the less formal H. W.

Dad kept Mama on the proverbial pedestal throughout their marriage. The pedestal was not always a comfortable place, because he tended to be overprotective and had a streak of jealousy. If another man had made a pass at Mama, he probably would have done so at the risk of his life.

Dad was contemptuous of any man who allowed himself to be henpecked by his wife. He was, however, amenable to subtle pressures, and Mama learned ways to cope with him without openly challenging his position as boss.

Dad was affectionate and emotional, while Mama was loving but, having inherited considerable reserve from the Perrin side of her family, was not demonstrative.

Dad was proud of Pearl, who dressed beautifully and "never had a hair out of place." He was pleased with the recognition she received from other women, who at one time or another elected her president of almost every organization she belonged to.

Dad and Mama filled our boyhood with security. One cold, clear winter night that I particularly remember, my brother and I, no more than four or five years old, were snugly tucked under a lap-robe in the buggy between our strong, protective father and beautiful, young mother. A full moon cast its reflected magic on Decatur as our pretty brown mare, Fanny, pulled our buggy from the square toward the Fort Worth & Denver railroad station. Henry and I, surrounded with love and warmth, felt great security, a feeling we kept until we were grown and away from home. There was never any doubt in my mind that Dad, if a situation should make it advisable, would have given his life for that of any other member of the family.

In 1916 Dad resigned as school superintendent, turned down an offer to teach mathematics at North Texas State Normal College, and went into the oil business as a promoter and eventually a producer. He said in later years that he had a wife and two young sons when he entered the oil business and either had $200 or owed $200 and did not remember which.

After he ventured into the oil business, Dad sometimes got up about 4:00 A.M. to drive to Wichita Falls, Burkburnett, or Archer City. Without awakening us, he kissed us goodbye. Sometimes we were in that mysterious state of mind between sleep and consciousness and knew that Dad kissed us.

When I was about four years old, I got the first spanking I remember. I had been unnecessarily aggressive in dealing with my younger brother, and my memory begins with Dad bending me across his knee and paddling me with a lightly rolled newspaper, doubtless a copy of the *Forth Worth Star-Telegram*. Dad asked, "Are you going to fight your brother any more?"

In my excitement, I thought he asked, "Are you going to quit fighting your brother?"

When I answered yes, Dad whacked me a few more times and repeated the question. I was trying to be truthful but decided something had to be done to stop the punishment. The spanking stopped when I finally answered no, but I had a guilty feeling. In later years I explained my dilemma to Dad, and he developed a guilt complex about the punishment.

Dad spanked us only a few times, and I really believe it hurt him more than us, though in a different place. After he spanked us, he took our pants down and massaged the area with Mentholatum. Mama spanked us more often than Did did and did not apply the Mentholatum, but her blows were light, and we learned to cry a little to get her to stop.

Some people think a child should never be spanked, that a spanking teaches nothing but brutality. The important thing, though, is the love and security a child feels. My brother and I felt such love and security that we could have taken many more spankings without suffering trauma.

Our family held occasional family conferences, some of which were arranged as punishment for Henry and me. In a "punishment conference" we reviewed our misdeeds and discussed future conduct. We preferred whippings.

We also had business conferences, in which Mama was in a weak position because Henry and I always voted with Dad. We should have listened to Mama carefully because she sometimes had superior judgment. In the late 1920's Dad had some good oil production. He proposed selling it and using the proceeds to pay for wildcat wells on land he owned in southwestern Wichita County near the present community of Kamay, a name derived from former land-owners Kemp, Munger, and Allen. When Dad operated there, it was called KMA. Supported by a three-to-one vote, Dad proceeded with his plan and went broke drilling wells too shallow to reach the deep KMA pool, which was developed a few years afterward and still produces. Fortunately, Dad salvaged some royalty, which provided financial security for him and Mama in their later years.

This improbable marriage of people from different parts of the country, of different temperaments, and of diverse ages was successful and lasted until Dad died, about six months before their golden wedding anniversary.

When I told Mama that Dad had died, she remembered above all his thoughtfulness. "A more considerate man," she said, "never lived."

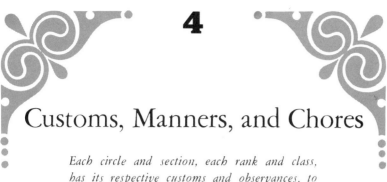

4

Customs, Manners, and Chores

Each circle and section, each rank and class, has its respective customs and observances, to which conformity is required at the risk of being tabooed.

CHARLES A. GASKELL

The settlers of Wise County brought their customs with them. Since most were descendants of pioneer farmers, the customs tended to be the same, regardless of which part of the country they came from. For example, there was a proper way to approach a farmhouse.

Dad's way of approaching a farmhouse came with him from Tennessee but was also standard procedure in Wise County. When I was a boy, I wondered why he did not knock on the door as he did in town. Instead, he walked to the front gate or within twenty or thirty feet of the farmhouse and shouted, "Hello!" If he received no response, he usually went near the barn and repeated the performance. If he still received no reply, we left.

The reason for this ritual was clarified in later years when I heard the late Crawford Martin, then attorney general of Texas, tell a story about an experience he had when he attended law school at Cumberland University in Lebanon, Tennessee. Young Martin had a job making weekly collections of insurance premiums on a "debit route." One afternoon he knocked at the door of a farmhouse. Having no answer, he walked to the barn, where fortunately he looked through a crack in the door before entering. He saw the farmer standing inside with a shotgun aimed at him and stopped immediately. The farmer taught Martin some manners by saying, "Bygod, don't you ever knock on the door of my house again; you stand outside the fence and yell hello like you're supposed to."

[37]

Another item of manners widely approved by settlers and the following generation or two was that children must be polite and respectful to adults. We learned both by stern instruction and by example to say Mr., Mrs., Miss, and Ma'am when addressing grown-ups. We were also told to open doors for women and to say please and thank you. Sassiness and insolence on the part of children were seldom tolerated.

A child who violated the custom of politeness and hospitality to older guests expected to be punished. When the family had company for dinner and the children were relegated to the second or third table, some children had difficulty in being polite. For example, my wife, Hallie, tells a story of an incident that happened in another Texas county over eighty years ago. Her Uncle Bill Orr and his brothers and sisters sat on a stairway anxiously watching through a door opening into the dining room as the adults, including the Baptist preacher and his wife, ate dinner. After the preacher had eaten an impressive amount, someone asked if he would like more fried chicken and passed the large serving plate to him. When the preacher took the last drumstick, Uncle Bill said in his big voice, heard by all, "Godamighty, there goes the last drumstick!" As expected, he later got a sound thrashing.

There were other limitations on children's expression. Dad gave special orders in regard to lewd writings on the walls of public toilets. He said, "Boys, you may grow up to be murderers or bank robbers, but please don't grow up to be toilet poets!"

While the children were restricted in expressing their opinions to adults, the grown-ups usually felt free to express their opinions of other people. In the absence of most present-day sources of news and sports, other people were often the subject of conversation. Some of the talk was uncomplimentary or was considered so at the time. A choice bit of gossip was that one of Decatur's best-known men had some years previously boarded in the home of another leading citizen, which apparently was true. According to the story, Citizen A was really the father of one of Citizen B's children. The evidence, less than convincing, was that the child looked more like Citizen A than Citizen B.

My favorite tale about gossip came from the son of one of the Methodist preachers, who lived in a parsonage near us and who wanted to learn more about some of the sins his father condemned. Wanting to hear the other side of the story, he soon discovered a rich source of information. Early on warm evenings he sat on the railing around the front porch of a little family-style hotel south of the courthouse square and listened to traveling salesmen (then called drummers) tell yarns. One salesman told a story about his cousin, who lived in the Red River valley, northwest of Wichita Falls.

That area, though flat enough to be surveyed into square-mile sections, was cut here and there by gullies. Easements often ran along the section lines, and highways, county roads, and little-used trails followed the easements.

One spring morning when the grass was sprouting and the field larks were singing, the rancher drove along one of the rarely used easements into a small gully and parked his pickup out of sight below the level of the prairie. He was proving his virility to his satisfaction with the cooperation of a woman from a nearby village, who was better known for her experience than her virtue, when both the rancher and his companion heard a car chugging along the easement. They looked up and saw the town's best-known gossip smiling at them. All three understood the situation clearly.

The gossip shifted gears, and her car leaped out of the opposite side of the gully in a shower of pebbles. As her car sped toward the village, the motor sounded like the hum of voices at the sewing club.

The rancher, a man of action, returned his companion to her little house and drove home. He greeted his wife affectionately and said, "Honey, it's a pretty day; come ride around the ranch with me and see our heifers." His wife, surprised at this show of interest and bored with housework, wanted to feel the exhiliration of spring on the prairie.

"Why not?"

As they drove through the pasture, she noticed that the grass was green again, that wild flowers were blooming, that the heifers were sleek, that some of them were frolicking, that the air had the aroma of spring, and that her husband was unusually attentive. She was filled with a sensation of pleasure, a feeling old but always new. Her husband eased the pickup into a little gully where he parked. His affection was enthusiastic and she responded.

About a week later the rancher went home one afternoon to get a block of salt for his heifers. When he went into the house, he found his wife laughing almost hysterically. He asked, "What's so funny, Honey?"

"At the sewing club today that gossipy old bag Mildred said you and widow Lucy Lou made love in a gully last Thursday, and I know better!"

So much for gossip!

Because of its prominence, the Waggoner family was a subject of conversation for many years. Dan Waggoner came into Wise County with the earliest pioneers and became wealthy. He built the Victorian mansion that still stands in Decatur east of the Fort Worth & Denver railroad tracks. Although the family moved away from Decatur, the people of Wise County enjoyed a sort of reflected glamor from the Waggoner success and publicity.

At Dan Waggoner's death, the *Decatur News* of September 12, 1902, published the following story:

> D. Waggoner, of Decatur, a pioneer Texan and probably the cattle king of the State, is dead. He expired last Friday night. . . . [He] came to Texas in very poor circumstances and lived to see his estate grow . . . to a vast estate, variously estimated as worth from $4,000,000 to $8,000,000. He was 74 years old. . . . It [the estate] comprises between 75,000 and 80,000 head of cattle and something like half a million acres of land.

When Mr. Waggoner's daughter Electra died in 1925, the *Wise County Messenger* dated December 4 described her as the beautiful heiress of Waggoner millions who had been born in Decatur. The

Messenger reported that she died in New York at the age of forty-eight after her brother, Guy Waggoner, made a record-breaking dash on a special train to be with his sister. According to the newspaper account, Electra had been married to Albert Wharton (described as a Philadelphia club man), Weldon Bailey, and James A. Gilmore, from whom she was divorced at the time of her death.

Sometimes families did things purposely to generate conversation, especially when they bought new cars. The thing to do was to drive the new vehicle around the square several times to let everybody know. When Dad bought a new Chandler and later a Buick, we made an extra circuit or two.

The courthouse square, a major center of activity, was especially important on trade day. As county seat, Decatur adopted the first Monday of each month as its trade day. The merchants enjoyed good business on first Mondays when the square was crowded with farmers who arrived either with money or with produce, livestock, or used farm machinery to sell or trade. An area near the square, called the jockey yard, was roped off for horses and mules. Professional traders, clever in their vocation, were often involved in deals. Neighboring towns in Wise County had to be satisfied with second, third, or fourth Mondays as trade days. In Decatur, as well as other communities, Saturdays were lesser trade days, without being so designated.

Cowboys from the country, generally from the Grand Prairie east of town, came to town on Saturdays, dressed in their best clothes rather than in their field clothes, which were later glamorized by the movies and clothing industry as Western wear. Barber shops then had a bathtub or two in the rear, and sometimes the cowboys paid the fees and gave themselves a good scrubbing. Also, they often got shaves and haircuts.

Some pioneer customs were observed in the country after they had been discarded in town. For example, a bride and groom in a rural area were often greeted with a noisy and boisterous shivaree on their wedding night. A crowd gathered around the house and beat on pans and tubs, shouted, fired guns into the air, and tooted

horns. The affair sometimes ended when the newlyweds acknowledged their friends. On other occasions the shivaree ended only
after the bridegroom was thrown into the horse watering trough and
thoroughly soaked.

Another custom was "pounding" recently arrived preachers and
new widows. Friends and neighbors each brought a pound or more
of something useful. Coffee, flour, milk, chickens, cake, meat, dried
fruit and the like were favorite items. The amount of food delivered
was frequently impressive.

Neighboring farmers often worked together harvesting wheat,
oats, or hay and hauling the crops to the threshing machine or hay
bailer. Other joint projects involved repairing of county roads and
cemetery workings. The latter were usually annual events in which
the women brought food and refreshments and the men cleaned up
the cemetery.

Fifth Sunday singings were conducted at rural churches, where
people came together for a full day of singing, eating, and visiting.
Serious singers sometimes went to singing schools where they studied the shaped notes of *do, re, mi, fa, sol, la, ti, do.*

Box suppers were a favorite money-raising device. Unmarried
young women packed suppers in boxes that were auctioned to young
men, who supposedly did not know who prepared the boxes. Each
young man, however, was well informed on the appearance of the
box prepared by his sweetheart. When a young man started serious
bidding on the box of his beloved, the other young men bid the
price up and made serious contenders pay dearly. The purchaser
shared the supper with the young woman who prepared it.

Other customs generally observed from pioneer times included
nursing sick neighbors, sitting up all night at wakes for the dead,
and preparing large quantities of food for families bereaved by
death. Also, neighboring women often assisted other women with
childbirth.

General customs were supplemented by special customs observed
by individual families. My mother, for example, dressed Henry and
me in beautiful suits made somewhat in Little Lord Fauntleroy fash-

ion, including pretty socks held up with fancy garters. Furthermore, we had bobbed hair that covered our ears and featured bangs across our foreheads. By appealing to Dad, we finally got our hair cut before starting to school. A rebellion was in order though, and my brother Henry made a daring breakthrough by using Mama's sharp scissors to cut his socks and garters into tiny pieces, which he hid behind a trunk. After that we had no altercations with our peers about our style of dress.

Some years later my brother and I had another problem in regard to clothing. We had long looked forward to 1925 because that year we would be old enough to quit wearing black-ribbed cotton stockings and trousers that buttoned around our legs just above our knees and ballooned down below our knees. Dad took us to Perkins & Timberlake and bought us each a beautiful suit with long trousers.

Our happiness with this evidence of maturity was muted, however, because that was the year knee-length trousers were abandoned for boys of all ages; even preschool kids wore long trousers. We felt cheated.

Chores for boys living in the country often ran into full-time labor, but town boys had it easier. Having no sisters, my brother and I had responsibilties inside the house that many of our friends with sisters did not have. We assisted Mama occasionally by washing and drying dishes. Often our work was not very helpful, especially when we scuffled around the kitchen and made slow progress. The house chore we detested most was scrubbing the kitchen woodwork and the white, enameled table and chairs. We also ran the vacuum cleaner and swept the kitchen and porches.

We liked outside work better; we mowed the grass, helped prune trees, cut weeds in the barnyard, and worked in the garden. In the allocation of duties, I was responsible for feeding, watering, and milking our cow, Old Jerz. She and I had a generally satisfactory relationship, although she occasionally kicked the bucket of milk over. Sometimes she swatted me with her tail, an activity I once tried to discourage by tying a brick to the end of her tail. She solved that problem quickly by swatting me with the brick. Although I had a close relationship with Old Jerz, she was more of a farm animal than a pet and had a mind of her own.

Henry and I were responsible for taking care of our pets, the most outstanding of which was our Angora nanny goat named Billy. We got her when Mr. A. C. Hoyl had a pen of goats rounded up and told us we could have one if we could catch it. That is how we got Billy, in a cloud of corral dust. She looked about half her normal size when we sheared her in the late spring, and she acted embarrassed about being naked. The gregarious creature was with us five years, but we gave her to a friend when we moved to Wichita Falls in 1926.

Other pets were a gray and white cat that had kittens and a terrier named Spot who moved from Decatur with us. Our chickens were not pets; their function was to produce eggs and fryers.

Children in rural communities in the first decades of this century, surrounded by pets and farm animals, probably had an earlier and broader understanding of sex than children get from urban street knowledge. They knew why Mr. Smith kept a stud horse, why Mr. Myers kept a fine bull, and why Mr. Cotner kept a jackass. They knew the difference between a bull and a steer and understood that a mule was a cross between a mare and a jackass and could not reproduce. They also were interested in and curious about the sexual relationships between men and women and eventually heard much of the local gossip about the affairs of some of the sexually aggressive adults. The Bible says that "from the beginning of creation God created them male and female" (Mark 10:6). This implies that there are differences between men and women, a truism long known to people in Wise County.

The boys in Decatur learned the four-letter words for various functions of nature at an early age and soon noticed that many men used these words in the sense of doing something *to* somebody rather than *with* somebody. They also learned that the four-letter words were not used in the presence of women or girls.

Henry and I did not get paid for most of the work we did, but one day, as a money-making proposition, Henry and I agreed to go

[44]

The 1908 graduating class of Decatur High School, including the author's uncle, J. R. Barton (*top left*), father, Henry W. Barton (*top right*), and mother, Pearl Perrin (*second row, third from left*), who was class valedictorian.

The Decatur Public School faculty in 1909 (*top*), including the author's father, who was superintendent (*second from left, back row*). The picture was on the front of the postcard (*bottom*) addressed to Miss Perrin, in which Henry repeated his marriage proposal: "Say Yes!"

The author *(left)* and his brother, Henry Will, in a photograph made about 1915.

In 1923 the Bartons' two-bedroom house was remodeled into this airplane bungalow.

The author (*left*), his mother, his brother, and little cousin Helen Ballard in 1921, the year Helen's father died.

The author stands at the left end of the front row in this picture of a grammar school class taken in 1918 or 1919.

The author with his favorite pet, a nanny goat named Billy.

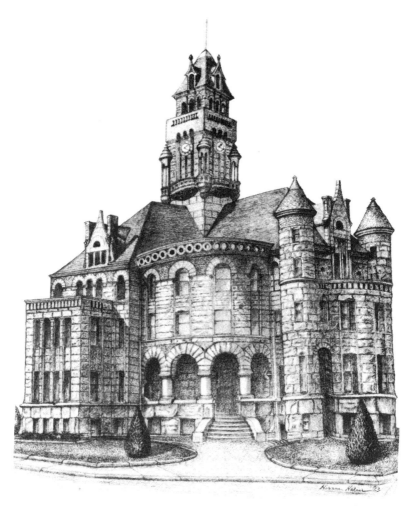

The Wise County courthouse, pride of many pioneers, was completed in 1893. Drawing by Hiram M. Helm.

The Woody cabin, completed in 1854, was the first home built in Wise County. Drawing by Hiram M. Helm.

This mansion was built by Dan Waggoner, a Decatur pioneer who became a millionaire. Drawing by Hiram M. Helm.

Decatur, proud of its notoriety, maintains this sign at its city limits.

with Mr. Lewis and his sons to pick cotton. Before we left, Dad told us he would pay a dollar to the one who picked a hundred pounds or more. When we weighed in late in the afternoon, I had about ninety pounds. Disappointed, I refused to get in the car when Mr. Lewis loaded for the five-mile trip back; I was still picking cotton when Dad drove out to bring me home. He did not say much to me, but he gave me a dollar a couple of days later for trying hard.

Johnny, the son of a Methodist preacher who lived in a nearby parsonage, had an unusual cotton-picking experience that same summer while visiting his cousins on a big farm in the Brazos River valley. He and his cousins played with several Negro youngsters, most of whom were children of "Aunt Jessie," a big strong woman who helped with housework except during cotton-picking time, when she and her family worked in the fields. Cotton matured early that year, and Johnny made some money picking cotton with Aunt Jessie and her brood before returning to Decatur for school. He worked along with Aunt Jessie and her kids, none of whom could keep up with her. She picked three hundred pounds a day, while pulling a cotton sack that served as a bed for her newest baby.

Once when Aunt Jessie stopped at the end of a row to nurse her baby, as she did several times a day, Johnny and the other children stopped for a rest. Aunt Jessie's oldest boy, about Johnny's age, said, "She's giving that baby chocolate milk."

"Aw, come on, George W., don't tell me that."

George W. offered evidence, saying, "Just you look at my mama; she's the color of them Hershey bars, and she's feeding that baby chocolate milk."

"Ain't no human gives chocolate milk."

"Ain't but one way you can prove what you're saying, Johnny; just go over there and try some of that good old chocolate milk yourself!"

When Johnny told us the story after his return, he still wondered if the milk might be chocolate.

My brother and I did some farm work for pay when we visited

Grandma in Haskell County. We chopped weeds out of cotton and operated cultivators pulled by mules. There was something humbling about riding behind the tail end of a mule all day.

Some customs of the pioneers and their descendants must have been puzzling to outsiders, as in the case of the farmer who was prepared to fire his shotgun at a stranger who knocked at the front door instead of shouting hello from outside the gate. Although early settlers were hospitable and often generous, it was sometimes difficult for outsiders to know whether they were about to be blasted or invited to dinner.

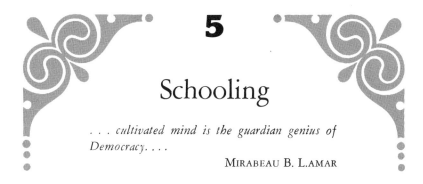

5

Schooling

. . . cultivated mind is the guardian genius of Democracy. . . .

MIRABEAU B. L.AMAR

The early settlers wanted their children to learn reading, writing, and arithmetic, but their understanding of the educational process was limited by their backgrounds.

Grandpa John Thomas Barton, a corporal in the Army of Tennessee during the Civil War, made occasional speeches at public events and was said to be fluent, but he did not read or write. Grandma Abigail Anderson Barton, born into a family of teachers and preachers, read the same book every day, the Bible. Their three sons and two daughters learned to read, write, and figure, and all three sons worked their way through college, largely by teaching, and earned bachelor's degrees. Dad, who became superintendent of Decatur Public Schools, also earned a law degree.

Grandpa James Perrin, who had learned to read and write before leaving Kentucky in 1853 at age fifteen, brought his school slate to Texas. Grandma Henrietta Gose Perrin learned to read and write in Decatur between 1860 and 1870, at a time when community activity was disrupted by the Civil War and Indian raids. Among other things, she was taught to say the alphabet backward as well as forward and could say it one way as fast as the other.

My parents went to one-room country schools, Dad in the Tennessee hills south of Nashville and Mama at the small farm community of Sycamore in northeast Wise County, Texas. The quality of their early education was not enhanced by equipment or facilities but depended on the relationship between the teachers and pupils. Fortunately, little country schools sometimes had intelligent, sincere, and dedicated teachers.

[47]

For example, Uncle Carl S. Perrin remembers Miss Austin, who taught at the Sycamore school in 1904 and 1905, as the best teacher he has ever had, and that includes college. She established discipline over several large, unruly boys who were almost as old as she, and she inspired the pupils to be interested in learning.

Uncle Joe Barton was superintendent of Decatur Public Schools in 1907–1908, when Dad was employed as principal. At the close of that school year Uncle Joe left Decatur to finish his bachelor's degree at Vanderbilt University, and Dad was superintendent for the eight following years. He did not tell us his salary, but a guess would be $1,200 to $1,600 a year.

Men teachers were called professor whether they liked that term or not. The local paper referred to Dad as Professor Barton the first year he was in Decatur serving as principal. The term was used by adults as well as students. Dad did not like to be called professor but was unable to change a custom so strongly entrenched.

In those days a school administrator or teacher in a small town or rural area often had to be courageous to keep his or her job. Some were driven away by violence or threat of violence. Dad was attacked once on the town square and emerged the winner.

On another occasion he was walking along a street about two blocks west of the square in the early evening, when a local citizen known for his strength and size announced, "I'm going to whip you!"

Dad asked, "Did you tell your wife?"

"No, why?"

"Because if you try to whip me, one of us will be left lying on the street."

Thereupon the bully reconsidered and resumed his walk to the square at a faster pace.

Dire threats were made against Dad at other times but were not carried out, possibly because of his success when attacked.

Some threats came from students. John Fullingim, a senior, was nineteen or twenty years old and larger than Dad when he decided not to come to school the next day. He announced his decision to his classmates and concluded by saying, "And if Barton says anything about it, I'm going right to the ground with him." Mr. Fowler, the school janitor, had a way of knowing almost everything that happened on school property and soon told Dad about John's threat.

Dad summoned John from a classroom and invited him to come to the office. John entered first, and Dad followed, locking the door behind him. Then Dad said, "John, I hear you're going to whip me, to go right to the ground with me. You'll never have a better chance than right now. Let's get started."

John reacted by saying, "Why, Mr. Barton, where did you ever hear such a thing? You're the best friend I've ever had!" And they were good friends thereafter.

In the first decades of this century, members of the teaching profession were occasionally called on to show physical courage. The attractiveness of a teaching career has suffered in many places in recent years because of the reluctance of courts to back up school boards that did not back up superintendents, who failed to back up principals, who did not back up teachers in matters of discipline.

When my brother and I were preschool age, a few boys who walked by our house on their way to school liked to tease us because we were the superintendent's sons. Sometimes they called us little girls, which irritated us, but we could do nothing except shout denials. One day a boy recited a little verse about Dad and Mr. Galloway, the principal: "Mr. Galloway went to town and bought a load of hay; Mr. Barton came a fartin' and blew it all away." The boy was disappointed because we were not angry, but we laughed and thought the verse was funny. We were careful, however, not to mention the verse to Dad.

When Henry and I were in elementary school, Decatur was populated mostly by pioneers, their children and grandchildren. Many of the old-timers were still there in the first three decades of this century. The usual attitude of parents was, "If you get a whipping at school, you will get another one at home." A less common attitude was that of a father who wanted to fight the superintendent or any male teacher who spanked his child.

Elementary grades in Decatur during World War I and for at

[49]

least a decade afterward emphasized reading, arithmetic, spelling, geography, grammar (also called language), handwriting, and deportment (conduct). Texas history and civics were taught in the sixth and seventh grades. Courses in high school were slanted toward admission to college and included English (with special attention to grammatical analyses of sentences, punctuation, and the writing of themes), history, Latin, Spanish, algebra, geometry, physics, and another science course. City schools had courses in woodworking and shop, but Decatur did not then indulge its students in such luxuries.

True-false and similar objective-type tests were not then used at Decatur. Examinations required either solutions to problems or essay answers. Students had to merit advancement before being promoted.

Teachers tended to treat all students the same, although some teachers tried to motivate students by counseling with them individually. Generally speaking, academic training was somewhat on a take-it or leave-it basis.

Our elementary teachers were typically single women who were lifelong residents of the community. Most were dedicated to their profession, had an intimate knowledge of the backgrounds of the children, and were short in academic training. They generally treated the children with understanding and compassion. Miss Ada Harding, Miss Belle Ford, Miss Maude Hogg, Miss Mattie Bates, Miss Frances Fullingim, Miss Johnnie Blankenship, and Miss Alma Christian were excellent teachers. The first five were teachers throughout their careers, and the last two later married and had families.

In the early 1920's we had a teacher from out of town who dressed flapper style. Her skirts were short, and although her dresses deemphasized her upper torso, they revealed a sensuous wiggle as she walked along the hall. A pioneer in the feminine rebellion, her hair was bobbed and short. We heard talk that she was a bad example for the girls and provocative to the boys. The school board did not invite her back for a second year.

Children enrolled at age seven rather than six because there were only eleven grades in public school, the twelfth being added later. I remember reading aloud in the first grade and suddenly losing my place on the page because I was reciting from memory. Although my class had very little arithmetic in the first grade, we were asked to add a few figures on the blackboard in the spring of the year. I added by counting on my fingers and did so faster than the others. When I wrote the total, the teacher, Miss Ida Shanks, kissed me. Although the kiss was a public commendation, I thought it was a public humiliation.

Both Henry and I skipped the second grade and thereafter competed with older children, a circumstance that did not cause any recognizable problems, except that later we were a bit immature for high school athletics.

Occasionally a teacher's compassion and knowledge of a pupil's background were tested to the point at which she lost her composure. One time a fourth-grade teacher, having been goaded almost to the point of distraction, called a boy to her desk and paddled him in front of the class. The exercise went on for several whacks, but the boy never cried or uttered a sound. He held a poker face and walked quietly back to his seat.

Paddling in front of the class was unusual, this form of discipline usually taking place in the cloakroom. Our building was designed with a cloakroom between two adjoining classrooms, serving both. It was a little hall the length of the classrooms with a row of hooks on each side for the pupils to use for hanging coats, sweaters, and caps. When someone was paddled there, the pupils heard a few whacks, a little whimpering, and then watched the grim teacher and chastened pupil return to the classroom.

I learned something about real education when my boyhood friend Walton Freeman treated me to one of my most satisfactory learning experiences. One afternoon he decided to teach me to count to a hundred in Spanish, having learned the language when his family lived in South Texas. He taught me to count from one to ten. He then told me how to count from ten to a hundred by tens. After that, it was easy to put the whole sequence together. The course in Spanish counting took place, along with play, in no more than an hour or two and helped me to understand how some children learned so rapidly in one-room country schools, especially when older children helped younger ones.

In Decatur, on the other hand, elementary-grade schooling in those years emphasized competition rather than cooperation, and we even formed lines for competitive reading. When a pupil made a mistake reading aloud, the one next to him toward the foot of the line was asked to read the same passage. The one reading to the satisfaction of the teacher advanced ahead of those judged to have read incorrectly. The object was to advance to the head of the line or at least to stay away from the foot of the line.

Once in the fourth grade I was looking out of the window when Miss Fullingim in her firm way announced that from then on no one would be excused to go to the toilet. The rule was more alarming than it would have been with plumbing equipment just down the hall. Both outhouses were at the bottom of the hill, with the boys going east and the girls west.

One spring day the reading line was formed against the blackboard on the east side of the room facing the windows on the west. We read the length of the line once, and several were "turned down" or passed by others. The procedure took considerable time, and, long before the last pupil read his passage, I felt an urgent need to go to the toilet. Remembering the teacher's firm position on the matter, however, I concentrated on waiting until the bell rang for recess.

After the last person in the line blundered through his passage, I was dismayed to hear the teacher say, "All right, students, let's start at the first of the line again." By that time I was holding my breath most of the time and also holding my water and hoping for the bell.

The boy ahead of me made a mistake, and it was my time to read. I knew the passage and was so pleased with the prospect of turning someone down that I almost forgot my plight. I took a deep breath to start reading, but having taken charge at one end I could no longer control the other end. I hung my head. The teacher and class were silent, but several leaned forward for a better view. Finally, the bell rang, and we filed out for recess. Neither my teacher nor my classmates said anything to me. I felt, however, that some classmates talked among themselves about my unexpected addition to the action in the reading line.

We sat at little desks made so that your seat was attached to the front of the desk behind you and the front of your desk was the backrest for the person in front of you. An inkwell was in the upper right-hand corner of each desk, and a girl with a long braid of hair occasionally had the tip of her hair dipped in the inkwell.

Once in the fifth grade the teacher, Miss Annie Plaxco, went out of the room. I took advantage of her absence to pull one hair at a time out of the head of the girl who sat in front of me; since her hair was not braided, it was easy to get hold of. Before Miss Annie entered the room, she stopped at the door to observe our conduct. She instructed the girl to pull my hair until recess. The girl was gentle, and Miss Annie instructed another girl to assist with the punishment. Girl number two, vigorous and dedicated, did a thorough job. Time passed slowly, even though the bell for recess rang in a few minutes.

Miss Annie had a niece in the class, Isabelle Hunt, who was smart and pretty. In my shy way, I became enamored of Isabelle but did not announce my feelings to her. Miss Annie, becoming aware of my infatuation, announced to the class that I was sweet on Isabelle, ending a romance of great possibilities.

Miss Ada Harding, my mother's first cousin, was my teacher in the sixth and seventh grades. She was ambidextrous and often started writing a sentence on the blackboard with her left hand and continued it with her right hand. Thus, she wrote long sentences without stepping to the right. She could also use the paddle with either hand.

Miss Ada, outstanding in teaching arithmetic, directed contests in which the pupils worked fast on the blackboard. Cancellation contests involving fractions were especially vigorous.

The windows had no screens, and houseflies sometimes came into the classrooms, especially on warm spring days after the boys and girls had eaten their home-prepared lunches. Some of us in the sixth grade developed skill in catching flies with our hands. Some flies got away, but we incarcerated a number in our inkwells. Once, during fly-catching season, my neighbor across the aisle, Dowden Dillehay, said, "Close your eyes and open your mouth." Being of a gullible nature, I obeyed his request, thinking I might get a piece of candy. He encouraged me to become skeptical by putting a fly in my mouth.

One day in the seventh grade someone put tacks in the pupils' seats. I sat on a tack, then noticed that the seat across the aisle did not have a tack and put my tack in that seat. When Miss Ada found out about the tacks, she asked each pupil if he or she had anything to do with the plot. Those who admitted guilt, all being boys, got a couple of whacks on the seat with a paddle. Not being part of the original conspiracy, I told her I was not involved; I have had a guilty feeling ever since.

In high school, which started with the eighth grade, we had a different teacher for each subject. Our history teacher, Miss Johnnie Blankenship, was excellent. We were seated alphabetically, which placed me on the front row near the big, round coal stove. One cold winter day when Miss Johnnie was out of the room, a girl named Milton, seated in the middle of the room, asked me to change seats with her. Even though she looked cold, I refused and have regretted it to this day. A few months later the girl died of tuberculosis, and she would have enjoyed the warmth of the stove on that winter day.

Our superintendent, Mr. Gill, was a strict disciplinarian. In the spring of 1925 I was sitting in the high school auditorium at general assembly. Mr. Gill walked along the front row of seats going toward the center of the room, apparently to make an announcement. Suddenly he grabbed the shoulders of a young man in the front row and jerked him to a standing position, tearing the desk from the floor in the process, and gave the young man a sound slapping on each side of the face. The pupil "took it like a man" and did not strike back or say anything. I did not hear what caused the outburst, but a good guess would be that the young man, who was about the same size as Mr. Gill, probably muttered something like "you old sonabitch" and misjudged the acuity of Mr. Gill's hearing.

Nearby Bridgeport was Decatur's archrival in high school sports, and football between the two communities was played with emotion. My brother and I were too young to achieve much in high school sports at that time, but we had a neighbor who was starting pitcher against a Bridgeport baseball team and acquired the nickname of "Mother's Oats" because Bridgeport "cooked him in three minutes."

Henry and I did not gradaute from high school in Decatur, because our family moved to Wichita Falls in January, 1926, the middle of my junior year.

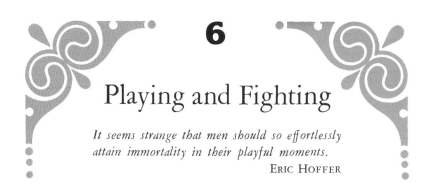

6

Playing and Fighting

*It seems strange that men should so effortlessly
attain immortality in their playful moments.*
ERIC HOFFER

As children in the early decades of the 1900's, my brother and I had many playful moments, but our play was different from that of today's urban children. Our play was largely unsupervised, even during recess at school. I wonder if our gains in resourcefulness might not be more important than the gains of today's children in techniques. Young people today seem to be organized, supervised, and coached by adults from the time they are four or five years old until they are grown. On the other hand, perhaps the regulated play of today's children will prepare them for life in the tediously organized society of the future.

My younger brother, Henry Will, was my foremost childhood playmate and is my lifelong friend. We were fortunate to be boys in an environment more closely related in matters of conduct to the nineteenth century than the twentieth. We were born only a year and a half apart, were sometimes regarded as twins by strangers, and were about the same size until he outgrew me when we were in our early teens. We argued, boxed, wrestled, played games, fought, and visited kinfolk together. Some of our play was dangerous, and we were lucky to grow up without serious injury.

Playing and fighting are considered together because our occasional fights were with playmates. We did not gang up on boys from other parts of town who looked or acted differently from the rest of us.

Our opportunity to play with little girls occurred before we were old enough to go to school and lasted only two or three years. At that time Audrey Tarlton and her older sister lived next door to us.

Audrey, about my brother's age, seemed interested in him, especially in telling him what to do. Henry Will, towheaded and cherubic, was obstinate. When he failed to follow her instructions, Audrey picked up whatever stick was in reach and whacked him. I once saw her break a lathe over his head. He did not strike back because Audrey was a little girl. Dad observed the situation and told Henry, "The next time she hits you with a stick, I want you to hit her with your fist."

Henry smiled as he said, "Yes, sir."

Soon Audrey whacked him again, and he landed a blow that shocked her more than it hurt her. She ran home in tears but began handling boys in subtler ways.

When we were preschool age and perhaps in the first grade, we went to birthday parties to which both little boys and girls were invited. We played games like drop the handkerchief and froggie in the middle. In the latter game, the children chanted,

> Froggie in the middle
> And can't get out;
> Take a little stick
> And poke him out.

For these and other games, the children held hands and formed a little circle. Songs for other games had words like "Go forth and face your lover," "Go in and out the window," and "I measure my love to show you." The high spot for the party was often pin the tail on the donkey, which was more of a contest than a game. Each child in turn was blindfolded and tried to pin the tail on a picture of a donkey attached to the wall.

Then, as though obeying some unwritten law, parents quit inviting boys and girls together to birthday parties. When we were too old for boy and girl birthday parties, the Tarlton family and their two daughters moved away from Decatur, and my brother and I found ourselves living in a neighborhood where boys far outnumbered girls.

About that same time Dad told us about a fight between two older boys at school. Lloyd Smith, who later died a hero in World

War I, went to Mr. Fowler, the school janitor, with a personal problem. Lloyd, spirited but small, was the target of taunts by Guinn Williams, who later gained national recognition as Big Boy Williams in cowboy movies.

With frustration and anger in his eyes, Lloyd told Mr. Fowler that Guinn was pushing him around and asked, "What can I do?"

Mr. Fowler, also a man of small stature, answered, "Eat him up."

"What do you mean, Mr. Fowler?"

"I mean bite him!"

Dad was then superintendent, and a few days later Guinn came to Dad's office bleeding from several wounds. After administering first aid, Dad asked, "Guinn, what on earth happened to you?"

"Lloyd Smith eat me up."

Dad took no further action. After that Guinn left Lloyd alone, and Lloyd enjoyed being left alone.

Classes for all eleven grades then in public school were conducted in the same building, which was about two blocks north of our home on a limestone hill denuded of soil and grass. That barren surface was our school playground.

The school had very little play equipment when Henry and I enrolled, except for a pipe supported by several posts near the east entrance to the building. The pipe, about three feet above the ground, had a high polish from its use by boys through the years. Among the favorite tricks were hanging head down from the knees and straddling the pipe and rotating around it. The girls all wore dresses and were too modest to perform these tricks.

About 1920 the school installed additional equipment, which lasted a few years. A giant stride was erected south of the building, and a sort of swing, which should have been called a battering ram, was constructed near the northeast corner.

The giant stride was a heavy steel pipe set firmly in the ground and rising about eight feet above the crumbled limestone. It had an axle sticking out of the top, around which could rotate a round iron plate from which dangled about ten chains with handles on the lower ends. The boys held the handles and ran around the pole fast enough to be lifted off the ground by centrifugal force.

Ordinary use of the giant stride became a little dull, and T. J. Elder had the idea of wrapping one chain counterclockwise around the others before the clockwise running started. The one whose chain lay over the other chains had a fast trip through the air above the heads of the others as his line sought its place among the radiating chains.

My brother, daring and strong for his age, was glad to take the first special ride. He gained speed and altitude quickly, lost his grip on the handle, and sped outward like a missile, which he was. I was playing elsewhere and did not see my brother's launching, but word of the incident spread almost as fast as Henry had been flung outward. By the time I found him, he was skinned and bruised from sliding over the gravel and rocks but was up and moving around.

The swing must have been made by the local blacksmith. It was a heavy two-by-twelve plank about ten feet long, suspended at each end about two feet off the ground by iron rods that passed underneath the ends of the plank and hung from steel crosspieces welded to two eight-foot joints of steel pipe planted firmly in the limestone at each end of the plank. Thus, four joints of steel pipe supported the swing, two at each end of the plank.

The swing operated like a battering ram and moved back and forth lengthwise between the vertical pipes. A number of children sat on the plank while two to four large boys stood at the iron rods and pumped the swing. It would be difficult to design playground equipment more likely to hit and injure or possibly kill a child who walked past the end while the heavy plank loaded with children was swinging with its great momentum. Fortunately there were no casualties, although my brother was once hit lightly by the plank when it was at the end of its swing.

When I was about eleven years old, Tom Pickett and I were playing at school when he called me a sonabitch and sort of grinned. I did not fight Tom, but I brooded about the incident because Dad had told me to fight anyone who called me that name. Tom and I were friends, and a few days later he called me a sonabitch again during recess. I landed a right to the side of his jaw, and we had a pretty good fight, to the satisfaction of the boys who quickly formed a ring around us and cheered us on. The outcome was inconclusive, but I do not remember Tom's calling me a sonabitch anymore.

A few weeks later I was wandering around the schoolyard when Furman Burton ran up the hill yelling at me. He said, "Henry Will and Tom Pickett are having a fight down the hill! Better come down and take up for Henry." The real problem was that Tom and Henry were not fighting enough to satisfy the spectators.

I ran down the hill and went through the ring of onlookers. Tom and my brother were facing each other in proper fighting postures but were not displaying much action. I stepped between the fighters and faced Tom with my fists up. Suddenly I felt a blow on my side, but Tom had not moved. The blow came from my brother, who later told me he did not want me interfering with his business. Tom moved into the spectator circle and watched with the others while Henry and I had our fight.

When I looked at Hannah Marie, a beautiful girl, the fact that my mother and her father were first cousins did not seem important. I was about eleven years old when the news got out that Hannah Marie and I were sweethearts, a relationship of which she was probably unaware. Unfortunately for me, the news reached Dub Stokes, a boy with extensive fighting experience, who was sweet on Hannah Marie. One day at recess Dub got his left arm around my neck, pulled my head down to belt level, and moved his right fist around in front of my face. When I was in that unfortunate position, Dub asked gruffly, "Is Hannah Marie your sweetheart?"

He gave me a little time to think about both my love life and my precarious situation. Reason prevailed, and I answered, "No, Dub, she's my cousin." With that announcement, he let me go.

We played a game at school called black man come through,

sometimes referred to as wolf over the river. Parallel baselines were drawn about seventy-five feet apart, and players in the middle tried to capture the others as they ran from one baseline to the other. Capturing consisted of slapping the runner on the back, which was done hard to get his attention. The running, dodging, and capturing continued until the bell rang ending recess or until all runners were caught. The players ranged in age from ten to the early teens. Blake Workman, quick and speedy, was one of the best players. The rocky surface of the schoolyard added zest.

Crack the whip was another activity. Ten or more boys held hands and formed a line, with the leader usually on the uphill end. The leader started the line going and suddenly moved back and then forward, starting a wavelike motion that accelerated as it passed down the line. When the wave reached the end of the line, it often broke the hold of the last boy or two and sent them tumbling down the hill.

Before frost in autumn, many country boys came to school with brown stains on their hands from gathering pecans while the husks were partly green. The stains announced the beginning of pecan season. Each boy searched for the hardest pecan he could find, brought it to school, and challenged others to pecan-cracking contests. A boy made a double fist with his fingers and hands, placed two pecans side by side in the double fist, and squeezed until one pecan cracked. The winner ate the loser's pecan. Some boys soaked their pecans in secret concoctions to make them hard.

The schoolyard was the principal place for playing marbles. The prettiest ones, made of agate, were highly prized. Other marbles were made of glass or ceramic material. We also used large steel ball bearings, called steelies, when we could remove them from old machinery. During marble season in the spring, the boys usually carried their marbles in cloth bags with drawstrings at the top. Some boys "played for keeps" and kept the marbles they knocked out of the ring regardless of who put them in. It was a catastrophe to lose an "aggie" in a game of keeps.

We also played with tops at school, and some boys were skillful at hitting other tops with their tops. A few even went to the trouble of replacing original points with screws and filing the heads of the screws into sharp points. Others packed lead into a hole in the center of the top of the top. The operator snubbed the end of the cord around a groove at the upper end, pulled the cord to the bottom, and then wound the cord round and round from the point at the bottom to the groove at the upper end. He then held the free end of the cord and combined a downward throw with a pulling back on the cord. The top rolled off on its side if the point did not hit the ground first with plenty of spin.

We played more in our neighborhood than at school. Our neighborhood was unusual in that there were just two girls, in contrast to eleven to fourteen boys, depending on which Methodist preachers were living in the two parsonages in the area. One girl, with good aptitude for football and other sports, was almost one of the boys. The other girl, pretty and feminine, was more interested in sportsmen than in sports. My recollections are mostly of boys playing with boys.

During World War I we played war whenever we could get several to agree to be Germans, and we played cowboy and Indians when we could talk a few into being Indians. Sometimes an imaginative boy, playing the part of an Indian, added realism by painting red streaks on his face with sap from a blood weed. We wore the grass off the Burton's yard playing one-eyed cat (a version of baseball for a small number of players), football, and other sports in season. My brother and I had a set of boxing gloves from about age ten on; the gloves eventually wore out from neighborhood use.

Houses then had barns rather than garages, and haylofts and barnyards were great places to play. We did daring things playing follow the leader and had corncob fights. A boy could really get stung with a wet cob.

A creek about half a mile away was a great place for exploration. We found an old lime kiln, caught minnows in a trap made of wire screen, and caught crawfish on pieces of meat tied to strings. Sometimes we jogged back home on the caliche gravel of the Fort Worth highway.

One night early in June the mockingbirds were singing, the air was so fresh it seemed intoxicating, and thousands of lightning bugs were flashing. The smell of spring was still in the air, and the kids in the neighborhood were stimulated. They ran and yelled as they caught lightning bugs and put them in little jars called lanterns. Occasionally one of us grabbed a lightning bug and accidentally smashed it, leaving luminous material that shined for a while.

After we enjoyed the lightning bugs, we played hide-and-go-seek. The one who was "it" hid his eyes (though sometimes not very well) and counted to a hundred by fives while the others hid. When "it" announced "Here I come with both eyes open," those hiding tried to get back to the base before "it" could catch them. The one who was caught became "it," and the game continued. This simple game among the lightning bugs was fun.

We not only enjoyed the hundreds, perhaps thousands, of lightning bugs at night in the summer, but we played with other little creatures of nature. A favorite was the little ant-eating Texas horned lizard, which we called "horny frogs." We picked the little lizards up by the tail to look at their prickly skin and the sharp, little horns on their head. They looked like miniature relics from the dinosaur era. Someone said horny frogs could squirt blood from their eyes when they were disturbed, a phenomenon we never observed. The unique Texas horned lizard (*Phrynosoma cornutum*) now has difficulty surviving in this time of spreading urbanization and insecticides. Under current Texas Parks and Wildlife Department regulations, "no person may take, possess, transport, export, sell or offer for sale, or ship . . ." a Texas horned lizard.

For seven or eight months we wore button-up shoes, black cotton stockings, and knee-length breeches. When the warm days of spring arrived, we happily discarded our shoes and stockings and went barefooted. At first the grass tickled our feet, but within a few weeks our feet were as tough as the soles of the shoes we had removed. We ran over rough rocks, jumped off shed roofs, and walked on the hot pavement around the courthouse square. Once I sewed two or three stitches in the tough skin on the sole of my foot with a needle and thread and did not feel any pain or see any blood.

We found it easier to climb trees barefoot than with shoes on. The best trees for climbing were in the Hoyl yard, where we especially liked to climb the mulberry trees when the berries were ripe.

A. C. Hoyl had a shetland pony and let us ride with him. Once A. C. and I saddled the pony, using only a single girth, which was not very tight. A. C. was in the saddle, and I sat on the horse blanket behind him. When the pony started trotting, the saddle flopped back and forth opposite to the way I was flopping. I fell on my head, and we tightened the girth before going on.

There were only a few black families in Decatur. Their houses were east of the railroad tracks, together with the cotton oil mill, the county fairground, and the historic Waggoner home, the most impressive mansion in the county. One day Joe Brooks, a black boy, wandered by our yard. We started talking, and he said we should build a little covered wagon, get some ponies, and travel around. I was impressed with the possibilities he visualized and his vivid imagination.

During the summer months no play was more important than running to meet the ice wagon. The iceman loved children and gave us little pieces of ice. The horse knew the route almost as well as he did. When there were two or three blocks between stops, the iceman sat on a seat at the front of the wagon to drive the horse. Otherwise he controlled the horse from the step at the rear of the wagon where he stood to saw or chip the ice and pick it up with his big tongs. The wagon was closed like a panel truck except for the rear, and sometimes the iceman let one or two of us stand on the step with him to enjoy the cool air.

Much of our reading was play because, except for homework, we read only when we wanted to read. We read about the adventures of Tom Swift, the Rover Boys, and Horatio Alger. We also read various other books and articles in magazines written for boys. Most of all, however, we read from two sets of volumes entitled *World Book* and *Book of Knowledge*, encyclopedias for children, which contained many illustrations and articles on countless subjects. As we grew older, Henry and I read other things, like books by Mark Twain and short stories by O. Henry. The two sets of encyclopedias, however, held our attention, and we browsed through them reading items that caught our fancy. After Henry and I read in that manner for a few years, we noticed a difference between ourselves and some of the children who did not read extracurricular material. School-work was easier for us, and sometimes we seemed to have an advantage that was almost unfair. We tended to run around with other kids who were readers; Walton Freeman and Orus Mooney sometimes exchanged books with us.

Shortly after Henry and I attained early puberty, Dad called us into the kitchen for a man-to-man talk about sex. He was uneasy but finally got around to telling us something about the physiology of boys and girls. We listened respectfully, as we always did when he talked to us seriously. He gave a sort of hop-skip-and-jump description of how babies are started and born. Then he told us he had an authoritative book on sex that we were mature enough to read, entitled *Sexology*. We replied in unison, "Yes, Dad, we've read it." He was somewhat taken aback; he must have thought we did all our extracurricular reading in the *World Book*. Unfortunately, our copy of *Sexology* has disappeared. It would be hilarious to read it today.

An important part of our play at home was making things. Henry was by nature a good craftsman. We got some tools from Dad and turned the former stable in our barn into a workshop, a fact evidenced by the sign "Workshop" that we painted and nailed above the window.

We made slingshots by tying two long and narrow strips of leather, one of which had a loop at the end, to an oval piece of leather cut from the tongue of an old shoe. We used the slingshot by putting the right forefinger through the loop at the end of one thong, placing the rock in the oval leather, whirling the slingshot while holding the ends of both thongs, and then releasing the thong that had no loop. We threw rocks long distances with slingshots, but accuracy was difficult. We often wondered how David hit Goliath in the middle of the forehead with such a weapon.

Our favorite weapons were niggershooters, and it never occurred to us there was a racial slur in the only name we knew for those handy weapons, hereafter referred to as shooters. The stock of a shooter could be made from a small tree limb that forked and was five or six inches long. The bottom limb was the handle, with the two smaller limbs forming a V above the handle. We whittled the best stocks, however, from white pine removed from the end sections of apple crates. We tied rubber bands, cut from inner tubes, to the tops of the two extensions sticking up from the handle. Then we tied the other ends of the rubber bands to an oval piece of leather that held the rock. These shooters launched rocks more than thirty yards, and we achieved considerable accuracy within ten to fifteen yards.

We made another type of shooter that launched an arrow cut from a shingle. We whittled a point at the thick end of the shingle and a tail at the thin end, and we cut a notch in the shaft about an inch behind the point. We tied a rubber band to the top of a straight stick and a string ending with a large knot to the other end of the rubber band. After placing the string in the notch on the arrow with the knot snubbed up against the shaft, we pulled the arrow back and released it, being careful to keep the point from splitting the skin between the operator's thumb and forefinger.

Pocket knives were our most prized possessions until Dad gave us shotguns. We even liked knives better than the Daisy air rifles we got when we were nine or ten years old. Dad broke the points off the first knives he gave us, a safety precaution we deplored. After we gained experience with the pointless knives, he gave us regular pocket knives with two or three blades. In addition to whittling, we played games called mumblety-peg and five hundred. We sat on the ground to play these games, both of which involved sticking blades in the ground from various throwing positions.

Present-day electric light bulbs are made of white glass and are filled with inert gas to keep the filament from burning out. When Henry and I were boys, however, light bulbs were made of clear glass, and filaments were prevented from burning out by a vacuum. A small, pointed tip was on the bottom of the bulb. Because of the vacuum, a bulb made a distinctive "pop" when it was broken. We enjoyed the noise making but soon learned we could hold a bulb under water, crush the small tip with pliers, and watch the water rush into the bulb. Then we had a water bomb just right for throwing.

One summer Henry and I decided to make a cannon. We found a piece of galvanized pipe about seven inches long and a half-inch in diameter, closed one end by screwing on a cap, filed a hole through the pipe forward of the cap, and mounted the result of our labor on a piece of four-by-four lumber cut to elevate the cannon about forty-five degrees. Ammunition was easy to obtain. We merely went to Lillard's Hardware with fifteen or twenty cents, bought some black gunpowder, and carried it home in a little brown paper bag.

The cannon was a great success. We poured powder down the barrel and packed it tight by forcing wads of paper against the powder by hammering on the point of a sixty-penny nail to drive its head against the paper. Then we poured some powder on the hole filed through the pipe, laid a piece of paper across the little hole, applied a match to the paper, and ran. When the flaming paper touched off the powder, the cannon roared louder than a shotgun and tumbled backward from the force of the blast.

The cannon worked well until one day I had the idea of driving the point of the nail into the packing instead of driving the head of the nail against it. We could not pull the nail out, so we decided to shoot it out. We aimed at the door of Mr. Nelson's garage at a range of about twelve feet and used a paper fuse a bit longer than usual. The cannon went off with its greatest roar. It exploded in all directions with pieces of barrel flying back over our heads. We did not find the big nail, only a rough hole about three-quarters of an inch deep in the seasoned wood of the garage door. We felt lucky and decided to turn our creativity to quieter enterprises.

Store-bought kites were rare. We made our own with slender

[67]

sticks, newspapers, flour paste, string, and knotted strips of rag for the tail. We adjusted the length of the tail to the strength of the wind.

Sometimes we tied a string to each corner of a handkerchief, then tied the four strings to a little rock, bent a pin into a U shape, and stuck the pin in the center of the handkerchief with the head of the pin toward the rock and the hook sticking above the handkerchief. Then we had a little parachute. We hooked the pointed end of the pin over the string of a flying kite and let the wind blow the parachute up the string until it was near the kite. Then we tossed the parachute off by snapping the string. It was a pretty sight as it drifted down.

We built a cart to be pulled by Billy, our pet nanny goat, who submitted to such an indignity reluctantly. The cart was just a box with an axle and wheels underneath, with a shaft nailed to each side to hitch Billy to.

We got axles and wheels from little wagons given to us at Christmas. We were often rough on our little red wagons because we wanted to get the axles and wheels to use in making coasters. We mounted two axles on pieces of two-by-four a little shorter than the axles by driving nails into the two-by-fours and bending the upper ends of the nails over the axles. We then found or sawed out a board about four feet long and six to eight inches wide, which was the chassis. We nailed one axle-equipped two-by-four to the rear of the chassis and attached the other to the front with a long bolt that went loosely through both the chassis and the two-by-four. We then mounted the wheels on the axles and fastened each end of a short rope to each side of the front two-by-four. We pulled the coaster uphill with the rope and then used it, together with our feet, to guide the vehicle while coasting down. We usually built a seat for the driver.

Perhaps our cleverest homemade toy was a little tractor put together from a spool, a tack, a piece of soap, a match stick, and a rubber band. During World War I we called the creation a tank. We notched the outer rims of the spool and drove the tack halfway in on one end. After we hooked a rubber band over the tack, we drew the band through the hole in the spool and then through a small hole in a flat piece of soap set against the opposite end of the spool from the tack. At that point we put the rubber band over the end of a match fitted into a groove on the outer surface of the soap. We wound the tractor by cranking the match around a number of times until the tension on the rubber band was strong. When we put the tractor on the floor, the soap slowed the energy from the rubber band enough that the little tractor moved smoothly and crawled over small obstacles.

We constructed a little device to make rope from binder twine, the coarse hemp cord used by farmers to tie ripe wheat together in bundles to haul to the thresher. We drilled three little holes about two inches apart through a board twelve or fifteen inches long. We pushed a heavy piece of wire through each hole and bent a little U-shaped hook on the end of each of the three wires, which extended through the front of the board. We then bent the wires on the back of the board into cranks, with the offset part of the three cranks being the same length and being flush against the board. We drilled three parallel holes, also two inches apart, through a second board and stuck the vertical portions of the cranks through the holes in the second board. Then we could turn the cranks in unison by moving the second board in a circular way.

When the rope maker was ready, we tied three equally long pieces of binder twine to the hooks, being careful to have the twist of the cords running in the same direction. Then we rotated the three lengths of binder twine in the same direction as their twist, making the cords tighter. Finally, under the scrutiny of the person holding the ends of the twine opposite the rope machine, the three lengths of twisted twine wrapped themselves together, forming a rope.

In 1924 or 1925 a device destined to affect the nation appeared in Decatur: radio. One evening Henry and I walked with Mama to the high school auditorium to hear a radio for the first time. I do not remember hearing anything but static, but it was wonderful.

[69]

Soon, Henry and I made a crystal set receiver of plywood, a Morton's salt box, a small crystal, and assorted other materials, including an outdoor copper-wire antenna stretched from the barn to the bedroom Henry and I shared. We spent many hours wearing the headphones and listening to WBAP in Fort Worth or WFAA in Dallas. Our special delight, however, was to tune in a station far away. Although we could occasionally hear broadcasts from Denver and once even heard a broadcast from Detroit, our parents seemed to regard our crystal set as a toy.

Some of our most vigorous play was on visits to the Perrin farms in Haskell County, where Grandpa, Grandma, and various aunts, uncles, and cousins moved in January, 1918, after selling their farms in Wise County.

On the visits, Henry and I played and ate impressive quantities of food. Our cousins, Julian, John Paul, Henrietta, Woodrow, and Jim (the baby), were children of Uncle Steve and Aunt Julia Perrin and lived a mile away from Grandma's house. Lake Creek ran through the two farms but flowed only during rains and for a while afterward and could hardly be called a creek, except in a West Texas sense. It was dammed in several places and had several tanks where we fished and swam.

Henry and I stayed much of the time with Julian and John Paul, who were our ages. They worked hard with their father, cultivating the land and taking care of the livestock, which included feeding and milking the cows. They had one milk cow that wrinkled her nose at us when one of us stood close in front of her and made an ugly face at her.

When we visited, Julian and Johnny were permitted to postpone most of their heavy workloads, and we played all day and part of the night. When Henry and I left after a visit of a week or ten days, our cousins were sometimes sick from the play schedule. If we had stayed and worked as hard as our cousins did, we probably would have been sick from the work schedule.

When Henry and I were ten or twelve years old and were visiting Julian and Johnnie, Uncle Felix Gose was there from Haskell.

He was very old, being the uncle of our seventy-six-year-old grand-mother. He had been a soldier for the Confederacy during the Civil War, having throughout that unfortunate struggle served in Missouri, where he was said to have been a member of Quantrill's guerrillas. He sometimes spoke of the "fighting Goses" and obviously thought the fighting spirit had been bred out of the family line.

Another visitor that day was our cousin Jewel Gentry (a boy) from Haskell. We were playing by the barn when Jewel started a fight by calling me a sonabitch. He landed a blow on my nose, which to my humiliation started bleeding. This show of blood was prima facie evidence that Jewel had won; I therefore had to make his nose bleed. He had a tough nose. Finally I got my left arm around his neck, pulled his face down to waist level, and hit his nose repeatedly with my right hand until it started bleeding.

At that point, Uncle Felix, who had been watching the fight with some interest, walked over and separated us. Perhaps it was my imagination, but Uncle Felix seemed friendlier to me after the fight.

Uncle Felix visited the Stephen Perrin family again about a year later. An expert with the ax, he was at the woodpile chopping wood for the kitchen stove when Julian heard the old man shout a long sequence of vivid profanity and rushed over to see if he had cut himself with the ax. When Julian arrived, Uncle Felix explained: "One night during the war I was about to freeze to death and went to a house owned by a Southern family to get a place to sleep. Nobody was there but a woman, who gave me a bed. Two or three times during the night she came to the room and asked if I was warm enough. I have just realized what she had in mind!" His reaction was fifty to sixty years late.

Our cousin Joseph Gose was a few years younger than the Perrin cousins, even though technically he was of an older generation, being the late-in-life son of our great-uncle Dr. Joe Gose. Nattily dressed and a great talker, Joseph came from Haskell to spend the day during one of our visits with the Steve Perrin family. During the noon meal he conducted a lively conversation while pouring molasses into his plate. He did not look but kept pouring while talking. Uncle Steve, however, watched the molasses calmly but with growing concern. When the level of the molasses was slightly higher than the edge of the plate and was held together only by its considerable viscosity, Uncle Steve asked calmly, "Don't you think that's enough molasses, Joseph?"

"Oh, my goodness!"

"That's all right, Joseph; just go ahead and eat all the molasses you want and leave the rest."

Uncle Steve and Aunt Julia were tolerant and understanding, but Uncle Steve imposed one rule firmly. He decreed that anyone who got mad at his opponent in a wrestling match was the loser. Sometimes after supper we cleared the chairs off the linoleum in the parlor and had wrestling matches. We learned to control our tempers.

Our play included the evening bath. In warm weather we bathed at the corrugated iron tank used to haul water to the house from the earthen tank on Lake Creek. The water-hauling tank was almost as long as the wagon that carried it and had an opening on one end that was big enough to allow water to be dipped out with a bucket. After dark we undressed and ran to the wagon. One climbed on the wagon, dipped water with a bucket, and poured it on the bathers, who whooped and yelled while pushing each other into or out of the streams of water. Our baths were more exuberant than thorough.

Henrietta, with four brothers and numerous boy cousins, spent much of her time in the kitchen helping her mother cook food to fill a group of growing boys and wash and dry the numerous dishes, pots, and pans. Later, when she started having dates, Henrietta said she had been around boys so much she knew what they were thinking before they said anything.

One afternoon Henrietta went to Haskell with her parents and Jim, the baby, and returned later than expected. They found Julian, John Paul, Woodrow, Henry Will, and me at the table eating whatever we could find. A large plate in the middle of the table was heaped with cobs from roasting ears, and a stack of six empty corn-flake boxes was in the corner of the dining room.

Uncle Steve Perrin had several greyhounds he used for chasing jackrabbits. Often the chase was between rows of cotton, where the rabbit could sometimes dodge through to another row just as a greyhound grabbed for him. Some rabbits escaped, but they were the exceptions.

One summer day Julian, Johnny, Henry, and I were playing on Lake Creek, and the greyhounds were with us. We saw a cotton-mouth water moccasin in a tank and threw large clods of dirt at it. We drove several moccasins, which were about three feet long, out of the water and onto the opposite bank. A greyhound attacked the cottonmouths one by one.

The dog leaped in, nipped at the snake, and leaped back just as quickly when the moccasin struck. This phase of action lasted several minutes for each snake, during which the greyhound displayed the perfect timing of a highly trained professional boxer. Finally, when the dog's teeth nipped into the cottonmouth, the greyhound shook the snake to pieces in seconds.

Henry and I have many memories of playing on our visits to the Perrin farms in Haskell County. We remember grandma's dishpan of sugar cookies, the neatly camouflaged nest of a nighthawk (which we called a bullbat), catching catfish, seeing Grandpa swim across a tank using a breast stroke while the water parted his long beard, shooting shotguns at cans tossed in the air, Aunt Julia's good cook-ing, climbing through a fence barefooted while eating a sandwich and seeing a water moccasin near our feet, shooting wasp nests with our shooters, galloping across a pasture bareback on an old plow horse at twilight and ducking instinctively when a low telephone wire flicked across the top of my head, seeing a coyote and hearing coyote music at night, running from a warm room and jumping into a frigid bed on the sleeping porch on winter nights and hud-dling together to get warm, having something of a fight with Henry one summer night because he objected when I crept up and poured a bucket of water on him and Johnny when they were sleeping in a wagon, seeing an old gray mule named Easter run in the pasture during her retirement after thirty years of hard service, seeing prairie dogs, getting badly sunburned once each summer while swimming in the tanks, stretching out on a linoleum floor with my uncles when they enjoyed a little relaxation after lunch before going back to the fields to work, running into the storm cellar when a cold front raced in from the north with a towering wall of brown dust rolling before it, and eating fried chicken and corn-bread and fried country-cured ham with biscuits and redeye gravy.

The foregoing account has little to say about boys playing with girls or vice versa, and that is the way it was, with the exception of Will Evelyn Burton, the neighborhood girl who played baseball and football with us. At school the girls jumped rope and played jacks. They doubtless did other things, feminine things, but they did not play with the boys. Girls happened to be scarce both in our neighborhood and at the Perrin farms.

When I think about the way we played as boys in Decatur, I almost feel sorry for present-day boys, who are supervised and coached by adults at expensive summer camps and in the little leagues of various sports.

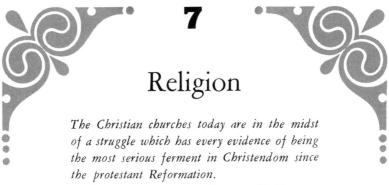

7

Religion

The Christian churches today are in the midst
of a struggle which has every evidence of being
the most serious ferment in Christendom since
the protestant Reformation.

JEFFREY K. HADDEN

Some of the religious customs of the frontier and the generation or two following that era may seem strange now, but many people of outstanding character and integrity were helped by the churches of that period. The emotional revivals of that time must have sustained some people whose lives were drab and burdened with heavy workloads.

Both the Methodist and Baptist churches came into Wise County with the pioneers as grass-roots movements. Part of the strength of those denominations in pioneer conditions was that education was not then required for the ministry. The preachers did not have to be trained in seminaries but merely had to "get the call." A man could be a farmer during the week and the preacher on Sunday. During my boyhood the preachers in towns were men with college training, but some of the rural preachers were men of meager academic qualifications who had answered the call, for which they must have listened attentively.

One summer evening when I was a boy, I sat on the front porch listening to Dad and several of his friends swapping yarns. Dad, a native of the Tennessee hill country, told the story of the call a neighbor received to preach.

> We had a neighbor named Charles who told several of his friends he thought he might be receiving a call to preach. One day Charles was plowing in a cornfield on the family's hillside farm. He was walking behind a mule and a plow when a neighbor quietly climbed high

in a hickory tree on uncleared land at one end of the field. When Charles turned the plow at the end of a row opposite the wooded area, the neighbor turned his face to the sky and shouted in a strong voice, "Oh, Charles, go forth and preach my gospel." Charles stopped, listened a few minutes, and, when he heard nothing more, continued plowing. Charles heard the same message the next time he turned at the end of the row, and he heard it several more times later. Finally, Charles threw the reins down and ran home without unharnessing the mule. From that day on he was a preacher of the gospel.

The Baptist church in Wise County was organized about a mile southwest of Decatur in 1855 in the home of Grandpa Perrin's parents. A few years later the Methodist church in Decatur was organized in the home of my great-grandmother Gose. In my family the Methodists won, because Grandpa Perrin joined that denomination with his wife, and they contributed twelve children to the cause.

The expression "shouting Methodist" was used occasionally when I was a boy, and Great-grandmother Gose, who died a year or two after I was born, was said to have been a shouting Methodist. She probably murmured a fervent "amen" or "praise the Lord" whenever a sermon inspired her to do so. During my boyhood, however, Methodists usually restricted their shouting to low-key responses, except perhaps at revival meetings.

The Methodists and Baptists had the largest church buildings and the greatest numbers of members in Decatur in the early decades of this century. The competition between the two denominations was keen, with a major difference being the manner of baptism. The Baptists had a strong selling point in the "once saved, always saved" concept.

The external appearances of the Methodist and Baptist churches were similar. Both were constructed along Grecian lines, were light in color, were two stories, had stained glass windows, and exhibited no cross or steeple. Both were solidly built and are still in use.

There were other denominations. The Episcopalians had a church in which the sanctuary was big enough for about a dozen people.

It was rumored that the Episcopal minister came from Fort Worth and played bridge with members of this congregation, an act considered sinful or at least shameful by many people in town.

The Presbyterians, Christians (Disciples of Christ), and Church of Christ had little churches. (In later years the Church of Christ gained impressive strength in the town and countryside.) A small Baptist church east of the railroad tracks served the several black families. There was also a small group, which we irreverently called the Holy Rollers, who spoke in unknown tongues and sometimes rolled around on the ground during revival meetings.

There was no Roman Catholic church in Decatur for Franz Gruen, an immigrant from Austria who must have worked longer hours than anyone else in Decatur. He baked at night and kept his confectionary and soda fountain open long hours six days a week. Maybe he went to church in Fort Worth occasionally. Even under these difficulties, he raised his family in his faith.

There was no synagogue for Mr. and Mrs. Cohen, who must have endured lonely lives. He was the junk man and traveled around the country in his wagon buying scrap metal and other items and becoming acquainted with many people. The Cohens had no children and were the only Jews in town. Mr. Mooney said he respected Mr. Cohen as a man of integrity, but I did not hear of any local people who were friends of the Cohens.

Mrs. Cohen once came to a Sunday evening service at the Methodist church. She became excited and started shouting, but not in the manner of a shouting Methodist. Several men from the congregation helped her out of the church and were gentle with her. I never heard what she was shouting about but suspect she was conscience smitten about being unfaithful to her religious heritage. She must have been terribly lonely among strangers.

My first memory of Sunday school was when Henry and I were in the primary department. Our mother and several other ladies conducted the class, where we sang little songs like "Brighten the Corner Where You Are," which we understood to be "Bright in the corner. . . ." We listened to Bible stories and always dressed in our

Sunday best. As we progressed, we were taught by two of the Hoyl brothers, who were prominent and prosperous citizens. Still later we were taught by Harry Halsell, whom we liked because he told Indian stories.

The primary department once conducted an Easter egg hunt under the supervision of Aunt Allie Gose. Her son Jarrell, who hid the eggs, watched the hunt. The children, equipped with little baskets, scattered in all directions, the weather being pleasant. Jarrell motioned to me and said, "Jim Tom, look by that fence post; look in that clump of grass; look under that little tree." He continued his suggestions, and my basket was soon heaped with eggs. I had more than all the other kids together. Aunt Allie, finally understanding the reasons for my success, made me divide with the other children, a requirement I considered grossly unfair.

When Henry and I were old enough to go to Sunday school, we were considered old enough to go to church. If we became restless during the service, Dad thumped our heads, and we quieted down forthwith.

We not only attended Sunday school and Sunday morning services, but we also went to the Epworth League, Sunday evening services, and often to Wednesday night prayer meetings. And once a year we went to revival meetings, usually to both the morning and evening services.

Although the churches had choirs, everybody sang. We were not just sung to, and the song leader paid more attention to the congregation than the choir.

The presiding elder of the Methodist churches in the Decatur area lived in the parsonage across the street from our house, and his son told Henry and me a story about his great-uncle, who lived in Calvert, a little town in the rich farmland of the Brazos River bottom. The old man had a fine baritone voice and sang in the choir for sixty years. He even sang at the yearly revivals, often called protracted meetings, where pressure was put on him to join the church and be saved. When asked why he did not join, he always replied in his fine baritone voice, "Because there are so many hypocrites in the church." He lived an exemplary life and continued his service as a major voice in the choir but never joined.

One member of the Methodist church at Decatur had a loud voice and loved to sing but had suffered brain damage and could not pronounce the words or carry a tune or keep time with the music. Although the congregational singing was unique when he attended, nobody seemed to complain to him about his determined efforts.

Dad used to sing an old church song to keep himself awake when driving a car late at night. He learned the song as a boy in Tennessee at a little country church that was too poor to buy songbooks. The preacher recited a line, led the congregation in singing the line, and so on through the hymn. The song went like this:

> There's a bright golden light
> That will lead us on our way,
> And it cometh from above.
>
> 'Tis the golden light of truth
> That will lead to win this day;
> 'Tis the light of the Saviour's love.
>
> *Chorus*:
> Golden light shine on,
> Shine on us from above.

Some sermons were about the end of the world, a subject no one can speak on with authority. Perhaps it was such a sermon that caused me to dream the world was coming to an end when I was eight or nine years old. In my dream, blue flames came out of the earth between our house and the cotton oil mill by the Fort Worth & Denver railroad tracks. The flames, though menacing, were not hot.

Then something happened that reminded me of my dream. I must have been nine or ten years old when one night an aurora borealis was visible at Decatur, a freak occurrence at that latitude. The school building north of our house was silhouetted against a sky that glowed red. The families of the neighborhood stood on the graveled street and looked with wonder. The Methodist presiding elder came out of the parsonage, studied the phenomenon, and concluded that the world was coming to an end. He returned to the parsonage and prayed at considerable length. His prayer was answered; the red glow faded away.

Sermons were preached on the seventh commandment—against adultery—with particular fervor, and preachers used to talk about the sins of the father being visited on the third and fourth generations. Dad quoted Scripture on this matter to Henry and me, giving as an example the physical damage to a child born to parents infected with venereal disease.

Religion had a direct bearing on the sexual activity of many people. The Methodist preacher's son once overheard his grandmother talking confidentially with another old lady. His grandmother said, "In all my married life I never refused to make love with my husband and therefore obeyed the Scriptures about yielding to my husband, but I never enjoyed it and therefore also lived by the teachings of the Bible not to yield to lust."

The devil was sometimes described in much the same way as he was often pictured, a terrible-looking humanoid creature with horns and a spike on his tail. Some people used the threat of the devil to control their children.

Once Henry and I were playing with cousins at Uncle John Gose's house and with a little boy about five years old who was the son of a lady employed to help with the cooking and cleaning. One of us told the little boy the devil was in the dining room. We were not prepared for his reaction; he was almost scared to death and started yelling and screaming. We told him we were joking and tried to get him to go into the room with us to see that no devil was there. He just screamed louder. His mother, who must have taught him to fear the devil, rescued him from his evil companions.

At an early age my mind often drifted into an imaginary world of its own during a sermon, a restful capability I still have. Once, in such a relaxed state of mind, I was sitting next to my brother at a regular Sunday morning service. The preacher was attributing all good, great, and beautiful things to Christianity. Henry, both attentive and disturbed, wrote me a note saying, "The preacher has attributed all great architecture to Christianity, but we are in a church modeled after a Greek temple."

The season of religious renewal at Decatur was heralded each spring at Decatur Baptist College. The usual compulsory daily chapel included plenty of warning about sinful living. Even so, some students were said to use profanity on occasion, to cheat on examinations once in a while, and even to fornicate sometimes, if rumor could be believed. Each spring a forceful evangelist, imported to conduct a campus revival, took over the chapel services and conducted prayer meetings in the evenings.

In the spring of 1928 the evangelist was hell-bent on saving every soul. The volume of his voice was impressive and his oratory eloquent. The fever of red-hot evangelism was contagious, and many students, especially those guilty of violating some of the Ten Commandments, wanted salvation. Early in the second week the evangelist was confident the students realized their hearts were black with sin and hence wanted to be saved. He shouted, "The Lord will save you! All who are saved, stand up!"

With a great shuffling of feet, everybody seemed to stand at once. The look of blessed triumph on the evangelist's face changed to a look of concern when he saw some of the students looking at two young men sitting firmly in their seats, one with his arms folded and the other frowning. The two, Perry L. Jones and Orus M. Mooney, were the objects of the evangelist's command, "Go save their souls!"

The song leader started singing, "Just as I am," and the students near Perry and Orus implored them to arise and be saved. Perry said "Aw, I'm all right. Don't worry about me; in a couple of weeks we'll be just like we were last month. Don't worry." He kept his arms folded. Orus continued to frown, because he was squinting his eyes to follow the flight of a honeybee that had flown in through a window and was wondering about the mechanisms that kept the insect steady in its flight. He scarcely heard the pleas of his friends and said nothing.

When the bell rang, Perry and Orus were relieved to go to Spanish class. When the class started, however, they discovered that the teacher and students were more interested in saving their immortal souls than in Spanish. The pressure continued throughout the remainder of the week, but the two young men were firm in their positions. It can be added that they demonstrated exceptional intellectual honesty in later years.

The revivals at the churches were customarily conducted during the summer. Dynamic preachers were imported from other places and conducted revivals, saved souls, and participated in special collections at the final service. The Methodist church owned a tabernacle across the street from the church building. The tabernacle had a shingled roof and was open on all four sides. A pulpit, an upright piano, and chairs for a small choir were on a platform at the front. A mourners' bench, a small platform about a foot and half high, was between the congregation and the large platform at the front. The dirt floor was covered with fresh straw, and the congregation sat on benches made of weathered pine. The benches had backs and were not utterly uncomfortable. The congregation tried to keep cool by using cardboard fans with wood handles cheerfully provided by the local undertaker as his opportunity to cool off the sinners and prospective clients.

In addition to the visiting preacher, the professional team for a revival usually included a song leader, who was also a soloist, and a piano player. Some of the piano players really jazzed up the old hymns. The team was assisted by the local preacher and volunteers from the congregation who got fired up and wanted to save souls. Methodists believed in instant salvation, confirmation classes then being unknown to most of the people in Decatur.

The tempo of a revival often started slowly while the visiting preacher studied the congregation and the congregation studied him. As the preaching progressed and the congregation's feelings of guilt rose, various persons became ready for salvation. When the revivalist sensed remorseful feelings among the listeners, he painted frightful word pictures of the horrors of hell, such as, "And the sin in his heart was as black as the soot on the walls of hell!"

Early in the second week some souls were usually saved, and members of the congregation pleaded with friends and acquaintances to go to the mourners' bench and be saved. The pressure was intense when the revivalist shouted his invitation and the people sang such songs as "Just as I am without one plea."

All seats were usually taken at night meetings, and a number of sinners often stood outside in the dark around the tabernacle. Some hardened sinners, however, brazenly sat inside and kept close watch on proceedings. For example, a rural mail deliveryman, who did not attend regular services, often sat about eight rows from the front next to the center aisle and added the odor of chewing tobacco to the fragrance of hay by expertly spitting dainty streams of tobacco juice. The crying of babies, a familiar sound at revivals, often stopped abruptly when the mother opened her dress and innocently started breast-feeding her child.

A powerful revivalist held a protracted meeting in the Methodist tabernacle in 1924, beginning the first Sunday in September. His sermons were forceful, and the *Decatur News* on September 7 of that year had a headline, "Evangelist . . . Drawing Large Crowds." Some twelve years later I was in the little West Texas town of Roscoe and heard that the same preacher was conducting a revival. Having nothing better to do on that hot, dusty, evening, I went to the tabernacle. The great preacher started his sermon by announcing: "I'm not taking a text tonight. That's the trouble with so many sermons; the preacher takes a text and then gives you his opinion about the text instead of giving you the real Scripture. Tonight I'm just going to give you the straight Scripture."

He succeeded in offering nothing but his opinions. After a few minutes I returned to the less distressing heat of the little hotel.

One revivalist announced to the congregation on a hot summer night, "There is just one part of the Bible I believe." The people sitting in the benches stopped fanning and looked at each other in disbelief, wondering if they had heard the preacher correctly. After a dramatic pause, the revivalist continued, "And that is the part from the front cover to the back cover." A look of obvious relief appeared on the faces of the congregation as they again started stirring the humid air with the fans so kindly furnished by the local undertaker.

Some revivalists specialized in denouncing certain sins. One, for example, gave considerable attention to the sin of dancing. His compelling argument was, "If it is sinful to hold another man's wife in your arms without music, how can it be right to hold her with music?"

Another revivalist said, "If a man wearing a glass eye should be dancing with a woman when his glass eye falls out, she would have to return it to him the next day after removing her clothing that night." I spent some time wondering about the physique of a woman that would make such a retrieval necessary.

On November 21, 1902, the *Decatur News* carried a story saying, "The Eidelweiss Club is preparing to entertain Christmas night with a reception and dance." Mrs. Mary Cates Moore (Mrs. Nob Moore) was a member of the club and later said it was disbanded because of local objection to the dances. The club was a victim of the numerous sermons on the evils of dancing.

On August 20, 1920, the *Decatur News* supported the revivalist's view of dancing by printing a syndicated article from which the following is quoted: "I look upon the jazz as one of the direct causes of the increasing tendency toward divorce. . . . No man or woman is normal after dancing to the music of a jazz orchestra for more than half an hour. . . . Jazz music produces a fevered disorder of the brain. . . ."

Another revivalist told the story of a woman who, having come forward to ask forgiveness, told him of a dream that bothered her. She dreamed she had died and was standing before the golden gate of heaven, which had four entrances. As she started through the first one, the ace of spades slid down and closed the gate. As she tried each of the other gates, another ace slid down and kept her out of heaven. Evidently neither the preacher nor the lady knew that she held a winning poker hand.

Revival meetings were sometimes reported like athletic contests. On April 19, 1907, the *Decatur News* announced: "The Baptist revival closed last night. . . . There have been 69 conversions, besides a number of backsliders reclaimed."

St. Paul advised, "Abstain from all appearance of evil" (1 Thessalonians 5:22). In the early part of this century, many families accepted this admonition literally and allowed no playing cards in the home, as though the cards were evil in themselves. The cards were considered bad because they were often used for gambling. Flinch, a card game that involved matching numbers in a special deck, was a favorite and was not tainted with sin. Forty-two, similar to bridge and played with dominoes, was very popular, along with the regular game of dominoes.

Carom boards were in many homes. The board, square and about the size of a bridge table, had a net pocket in each corner. The caroms, made of wood, were doughnut shaped and about an inch wide. The players thumped the "taws" against other caroms attempting to knock them into the pockets. Carom resembled pool, a game many considered to be sinful.

It would not be fair for me to blame the Methodist church for my ineptness at cards or dancing, because I later went to that focal point of Christian education, Southern Methodist University, and learned to enjoy both alleged vices.

In 1925, the Scopes trial in Tennessee had a strong impact in Decatur, where William Jennings Bryan was a folk hero. People said: "The very idea, saying we are descended from monkeys! All you need to do to understand how man and woman were created is to read Genesis."

Orus Mooney, then about sixteen years old, announced that he believed there might be some truth in what Mr. Scopes was teaching. For his courageous statement, Orus was nicknamed Jocko, a common name for a monkey in those days. Orus was later threatened with expulsion from Decatur Baptist College for insisting on reading H. G. Wells's *Outline of History*, which comments favorably on the Darwinian theory. Just for the heck of it, Orus announced his own theory, namely, that God created man, and other forms of life evolved from him.

On May 5, 1927, the *Wise County Messenger* carried this story, which met with considerable local approval: "Dr. J. Frank Norris, pastor of the First Baptist Church in Fort Worth, and one of the best known preachers in the south, will deliver three sermons at the Methodist tabernacle. . . . Dr. Norris is editor of *The Fundamentalist*, a weekly publication that is making war on all those who preach evolution. Dr. Norris says he believes the Bible from cover to cover and has no patience with the high brow theological experts who claim that man sprang from tadpoles and monkeys. . . ."

A few years after we moved away from Decatur, my friend Orus Mooney taught in a one-room country school to earn enough money for another year in college. As customary, he was drafted for extra duties, including that of teaching Sunday school.

A member of the church, a hard-working and successful young farmer, drove to town one afternoon. Although the sun was bright, a norther chilled the countryside. The farmer offered a ride to a young lady who was walking toward town, even though he knew her reputation, which entertained concern as to her morals. The trip was uneventful, and the farmer let the young lady out on the courthouse square. Her arrival was noted by the gentlemen who sat on the courthouse steps and chewed tobacco.

The young lady told an acquaintance the young farmer had made an immoral proposition when she was in the car with him. This bit of scandal spread rapidly and was known to some members of the farmer's congregation before he returned home. By the following Sunday the whole congregation, informed of their member's scandalous conduct, was prepared to expel him from membership.

In the meantime, Mooney, having heard of the plot to expel his friend, prepared a special Sunday school lesson based on the second sentence of the seventh verse of the eighth chapter of St. John, namely, "He that is without sin among you, let him cast the first stone." Mooney made a strong talk at Sunday school and concluded by withdrawing his letter of membership and resigning from the congregation. Almost fifty years later the farmer remains a member of the church, but Mooney has not yet placed his letter with another congregation.

[86]

At that time of religious fundamentalism, one respected citizen, a man whose business was on the courthouse square, never went to church. He neither spoke to others about his beliefs nor challenged their beliefs. He was sometimes the subject of conversation among his friends concerning his prospects of going to heaven. Through it all, he lived such an upright and exemplary life that no one had the courage to question his beliefs.

The Methodist church used to move its preachers every two years or so. With such a rapid turnover, it is difficult to remember individuals. The Reverend J. W. Slagle was a fine preacher, and the Reverend Harrison Baker was outstanding in character, intelligence, and compassion. Dr. Robert E. Bell was pastor of the Baptist church for many years, and he would have been outstanding for any congregation. He was courageous, effective in the pulpit, and sincere in his concern for his church and community.

Dad's funeral was conducted at the United Methodist church at Decatur in 1958, and the family had a good look at the church and churchyard for the first time in thirty-two years. The original building appeared much the same as in earlier years, but in other respects there were obvious changes. The name had been changed; when we moved away in 1926, it had been the Methodist Episcopal Church South. An education building had been added to the rear of the church; the tabernacle across the street had been replaced by a parking lot; and a picture of Jesus on glass with an electric light behind it was above the pulpit. The last two of the changes would have been unacceptable several decades earlier.

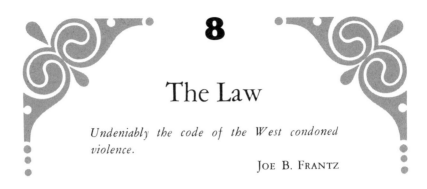

8

The Law

Undeniably the code of the West condoned violence.

JOE B. FRANTZ

The citizens of Wise County have not taken enforcement of the law into their own hands except on one occasion during the Civil War, when five white Union sympathizers were hanged from a tree at the west edge of town after a "trial." Grandma Perrin, then a young girl, remembered seeing the Union sympathizers in wagons, sitting on their coffins as horses pulled the unfortunate members of the "peace party" westward from the village square.

Racial strife in the early days was largely limited to the militant relationship between white men and Indians. Although there is no record of the lynching of a black in Decatur, newspaper reports of lynchings in other places tended to be slanted against blacks. For example, the *Decatur News* on October 10, 1902, reported that the lynching of Ot Duncan at Columbus, the county seat of Colorado County, had been done by some 125 of Eagle Lake's leading citizens.

Decatur people respected the authority of the sheriff, his deputies, and the town constable. Lawbreakers, advised of no civil or constitutional rights, were handled in a way considered appropriate by the arresting officer. When someone said "the law," he usually referred to a police officer rather than statutes and court decisions.

An old-timer once told me a yarn about a criminal investigation made in the 1890's by a lawman. A deputy rode his horse about eight miles northwest of town to investigate the burglary of a farmhouse. When he arrived, he looked around the house and barnyard without making any comment. Finally he asked the farmer, "Where's your dog?"

"Ain't got one."

"Bygod, anybody too stingy to keep a dog ought to be robbed." With that statement, the deputy closed the case and rode back to town.

Early in this century the arrest of horse thieves was headline material for the *Decatur News*, as when it announced on May 23, 1913, "Horse Thieves Arrested in Decatur," and again on November 10, 1914, when it headlined, "Horse Thief Captured in Short Order."

When some men broke out of the Decatur jail in 1920, the report in the July 16 *Decatur News* indicated that among the crimes for which they had been arrested, theft of automobiles had replaced horse stealing as a common crime:

Theft of car	4
Rape	1
Forgery	1
Burglary	1
TOTAL	7

A person who stole a horse, cow, or car could not expect to receive the same understanding as a person who committed homicide. A citizen who killed someone "in defense of his home" was more likely to be regarded as a hero than a criminal.

For example, on March 6, 1925, the *Wise County Messenger* reported that: "Jim Wells, living on East Walnut Street, gave an unwelcome visitor at his home a warm reception early Wednesday morning, when he fired through the front door of his home in response to an intruder's efforts to break in the door."

The Spencer murder was a more extreme situation. When my brother and I were young boys, the most talked-about homicide was the Spencer case, which must have happened between 1914 and 1918, a period for which most of the copies of the *Decatur News* and the *Wise County Messenger* are missing.

Uncle Carl Perrin and my brother remember the murder this way. Mr. Spencer, a respected Decatur citizen, had marital problems, and his wife took the children and went to her mother's home in Waco. Spencer, anxious to make up, wrote his wife, and asked her to meet him in Fort Worth to try to effect a reconciliation. He suggested a time and place for the proposed meeting.

The post office delivered the letter to the wrong address in Waco, where it was opened and read by a married man of an insanely jealous nature. The man, hereafter called Mr. Doe, confronted his wife and charged her with arranging to meet the unknown Spencer for a tryst in Fort Worth.

Ignoring his wife's hot denials, Doe pocketed a pistol and traveled to Decatur, where he went to the courthouse square, inquired about Spencer, and got a description. Doe saw someone similar to the description and asked a man passing by, "Is that Spencer?" On receiving an affirmative answer, Doe drew his pistol and, without warning, shot Spencer in the back, killing him.

What appeared to be a premeditated, cold-blooded, and cowardly murder was found by the jury to be an act of protection of Doe's home, and he was found not guilty.

As provided by local option, the citizens of Decatur outlawed the sale of alcoholic beverages early in this century. Whiskey was sold illegally, but it was whiskey manufactured in legitimate distilleries and smuggled into Decatur from Fort Worth. The enactment of nationwide prohibition, however, closed the distilleries and created a new class of criminal, the bootleg whiskey maker.

Reports of raids by lawmen on stills and their operators appeared in the March 31, 1921, and May 21, 1921, issues of the *Decatur News* and in the May 12, 1921, and November 30, 1923, issues of the *Wise County Messenger*. Perhaps the most impressive still captured in 1921 was reported in the following manner: "They found the still in full operation, just pulling off a run of 15 gallons of pure corn juice. . . . The still was made of a big milk can and the worm [meaning the condensing coil] looked like it had been made from tubing taken from an automobile, Sheriff Malone said."

The editor of the *Wise County Messenger* was said by friends to study the effects of corn whiskey on his occasional trips to Dallas. Even so, he pleased many of his constituents by using a murder trial as an excuse to editorialize against bootleg liquor, in an article ostensibly reporting the court proceedings.

The unfortunate homicide was headlined on December 14, 1923, as "Kirby Kills Bill Covington." As the story developed in later issues, the Kirby and Covington families were longtime friends who lived on adjoining farms in the vicinity of Greenwood in northeast Wise County. One evening when Mr. Kirby and Mr. Covington were playing dominoes and drinking whiskey together at the Kirby home, they became involved in an argument. Kirby's son, about twenty-two years old, shot Mr. Covington, possibly because young Kirby overestimated the seriousness of the disagreement.

Under the headline "Kirby Trial Attracts Crowd," the *Wise County Messenger* on January 25, 1924, featured the following story:

> The Kirby and Covington families were neighbors in the Greenwood-Slidell community. Living a short distance apart, the members of the two families exchanged visits almost daily. The Covington children and the Kirby children played with one another. Mrs. Covington and Mrs. Kirby were warm friends, and their husbands were boon companions. Kirby and Covington worked together, and, they drank together. And this drinking together—this neighborly spreeing and bringing into play the fruit jars with their contents of reason destroying and brain robbing liquid—killed that love and affection existing between the families, arrayed neighbor against neighbor, brought sorrow and hate to overthrow happiness and good cheer. It robbed a wife of her husband, created orphans, and dyed the hands of a stalwart youth with the blood of his fellow man. Mothers are bowed and groping in a black night; a father is staggering beneath a burden of sorrow; and grief's dark clouds have dissipated happiness in the hearts of brothers and sisters; children are wide-eyed, wondering, wondering and prattling babies goo inquiries.
>
> Whiskey's frightful score!

After a trial, lasting five days, young Kirby was found not guilty because ". . . it was claimed by the defendant that he shot and killed Covington while defending his father against the attacks of Covington." The jury deliberated five minutes.

The Perrin family never had any trouble with the law, but the youngest son, Clarence, had a close call in 1924. He and several other young men, including Bert Davis from Dad's side of the family, tried to find a little excitement one night and decided to steal some wine from Henry Vandiver, a farmer known for his skill in making mustang-grape wine for home use. The problem was that Mr. Vandiver, armed with his shotgun, caught the intruders, who were in danger of being charged with breaking and entering and conspiring to transport and use a prohibited substance. Mr. Vandiver, whose sister was the wife of Stephen Perrin, one of Clarence's older brothers, did not file charges.

The most memorable thing about the wine incident in the Barton household was the way Dad broke the news to Mama. As Mama was starting up the steps to the bedrooms in our new airplane bungalow, Dad said, "Pearl, some young men were caught trying to break in and steal Henry Vandiver's wine."

Mama, a dedicated prohibitionist and member of the Women's Christian Temperance Union, said, "Well, they should just be sent to the penitentiary."

"One of them was your brother Clarence."

Mama' face turned red, and she walked up the steps without saying another word.

Decatur's weekly papers printed more stories about arrests than convictions, and a lawman's authority to arrest was impressive. For example, on February 19, 1924, the *Wise County Messenger* had a headline saying, "Prowling Stranger Picked up by Deputy." According to the report, "Deputy Sheriff George Gage arrested a stranger on suspicion and put him in jail." Obviously, a stranger in Decatur should not have acted suspiciously.

On May 16, 1924, the same paper had as a headline, "Officers Stop Petting Party—Rounders with Gay Girls Fined." (The word *gay* did not have its present connotation.) The story was: "Deputy Sheriffs . . . were called . . . to look after the conduct of two men and two women, who it was reported were staging petting parties along the road. The officers arrested two young men and a couple of women."

On July 6, 1924, a different and locally unknown human condition was announced to Decatur when the *Messenger* printed the following story about a transvestite: "He-flapper gets in jail. George Hart of New York was arrested as he changed from girl's apparel to overalls . . . one of the vilest mouthed prisoners that has been in the county jail in many years." Nobody appeared concerned about Mr. Hart's rights.

The excessive force sometimes used by policemen was not confined to criminals but was on occasion used on ordinary citizens arrested for traffic violations. The *Messenger* of November 10, 1925, carried a story under the headline "Jitney Driver Attacked by Officer Bully." (The word *jitney*, commonly used in the 1920's, is defined as "a small bus that carries passengers over a regular route according to a flexible schedule.") The story, about a brutal attack by a Fort Worth policeman on a man from nearby Denton who was arrested for speeding, read as follows:

> Ira T. Burton was arrested for speeding by officer Olman in North Fort Worth on his run to Denton. Olman ordered Burton (who had passengers in his car) to drive him to the city hall. Burton stopped his car and asked if he could take his passengers to the bus line headquarters. Burton got out of the car on Olman's orders and Olman hit him on the head with his night stick, fracturing Burton's skull. Passengers said Olman made a savage attack and would testify to that effect.

Lawmen in Decatur, however, usually understood the local people and had a sense of humor. Mr. Mooney, Orus' father, was a scrapper, all 150 pounds of him. Mooney became angry at a member of the school board for keeping his boys from going to school when the Mooney home was quarantined. On finding the board member at Dick Reeves' barber shop, Mooney pummeled him with a few blows, and the board member ran out the back door. Mooney, one to get along with the law, walked to the sheriff's office to pay his fine. The sheriff laughed and said, "Mooney, we don't have any charge against you, but we may arrest that school board man for speeding."

9

Secret Organizations

*For thou did it secretly; but I did this thing
before all. . . .*

II SAMUEL 12:12

Two or three years after the end of World War I a secret organization appeared in Decatur and much of the South that proposed to substitute its form of punishment for forms approved by the courts. The Ku Klux Klan (KKK) apparently planned to protect Decatur from Catholics, Jews, and Negroes. Such a mission should have been simple in Decatur, which had one Catholic family, one Jewish couple, and only a few black families.

On September 22, 1921, the *Decatur News* printed this letter, reportedly left on a table in a local "sinful joint" by an unknown person:

> Knights of the Texas Ku Klux Klan—Invisible Impire, Township Den of Decatur.
>
> Sept. 23, 1921
>
> To Whom it May Concern:
>
> WE, the Knights of the Ku Klux Klan of Texas, hereby announce our presence in the city of Decatur, county of Wise, State of Texas, this 23rd day of September, 1921. We issue this script as a warning to all evil-doers in general and one in particular, who have been guilty of various and sundry misdemeanors of late and have not been apprehended, that such conduct will be tolerated no longer. We warn only once. At the second offense WE ACT.
>
> KNIGHTS OF THE KU KLUX KLAN
> Borne by the Knighthawk
>
> Please Post.
> Grand Scribe.

An interesting point is that the date of the paper that published the proclamation was one day prior to the date on the proclamation.

Many men joined the KKK because of the urging of their friends. Others joined because of fascination with the white robes and the secrecy or misdirected feelings of community action. Others paid their money and were initiated but never went to another meeting after they realized that the Klan proposed to substitute its ideas of conduct and its versions of punishment for those of the courts and law enforcement agencies.

It must have been in the autumn of 1921 that a large meeting of the Klan was held after dark on the prairie east of Decatur. Almost everybody in town knew about the meetings, and many wives and children drove out to watch the proceedings from a distance. Mama drove Henry Will and me to the vantage point, where many cars were parked. Klansmen patrolled the barbed wire fence around the pasture where the meeting was held. Suddenly a large cross flamed impressively, and we saw white-robed men beyond it. We did not know what they were doing but heard later that the officers were initiating new members.

My brother and I did not know it at the time, but Dad was in the group being initiated, having come to the meeting at the urging of friends and former students. Dad returned from the initiation disillusioned about the Klan, its objectives, and its methods of operation. He became openly critical of the organization and never attended another meeting. As a nonbeliever in the KKK, he received several threats and had some concern for the safety of the family and himself.

One night a car stopped in front of the house, and the driver honked the horn. Dad, thinking of possible retribution from the Klan, slipped his .32 Smith & Wesson revolver in his pocket before going out. The driver was just a friend who wanted Dad to see his new car.

Some preachers were openly critical of the Klan, which created a problem for an organization that professed to sponsor virtue and clean living. Other preachers directed their sermons against various sins and did not mention "political" subjects like the Klan. Sometimes they were rewarded for their lack of perception and courage. Mama once took Henry and me to a revival meeting in the country a few miles from town. The meeting was in a brush arbor, in which the roof consisted of fresh tree branches rather than shingles. We were surprised at the end of the service when two Klansmen, who must have been selected for their height, walked down the aisle with slow, steady strides and handed the preacher an envelope said to contain fifty dollars.

Years afterward Henry and I heard about the courage of another man at the big initiation. Mr. R. L. Hunt, having been urged by his friends to join, replied, "All right, I'll join if I don't have to agree to something I don't believe in." On the assurance of his friends, he went to the initiation. While the oath of membership was being administered, Mr. Hunt stepped out of the group and said, "I can't agree to that."

All eyes turned to Mr. Hunt as he stood distinctly away from the group being initiated. The Klansmen, most of them lifetime acquaintances, threatened him with physical harm. Mr. Hunt, firm in his decision, walked out of the pasture past the robed figures, and nobody stopped him.

A year or two later Mr. Hunt and his family were attending a Sunday evening service at the Baptist church when four robed Klansmen came in just as the congregation sat in the pews after finishing a hymn. As the Klansmen strode down the aisle toward the pulpit, Isabelle Hunt, then eleven or twelve years old, was sitting by her father and, snuggling closer when she saw the robed men, said, "Daddy, I'm scared."

Her father replied calmly, "Honey, they won't hurt you; they're cowards."

In the meantime, Dr. Robert E. Bell, pastor, sized up the situation. He was openly critical of the Klan and had heard rumors that he was to be "put in his place." The four robed Klansmen marching down the aisle probably had a plan to do just that.

When the Klansmen were near some empty pews, Dr. Bell announced calmly, "We will stand for prayer." He delivered a prayer appropriate to the occasion and said, "The congregation will be seated." The Klansmen were left standing in the aisle, and Dr. Bell said to them firmly, "Gentlemen, you will please be seated for worship." They sat meekly through the sermon.

Isabelle Hunt, as a child, had still another experience with the Klan. She suspected that an uncle who lived in nearby Fort Worth was a member of the KKK. Her suspicion became greater when her uncle appeared at their home for supper on the same evening that a Klan rally and parade had been announced.

During supper, Isabelle excused herself from the table, went to her room, and got a piece of chalk. On returning to the table, she dropped the chalk on the floor in such a way that it rolled under the table. She then crawled under the table to retrieve the chalk and marked an "X" on one of her uncle's black shoes. Later that evening at the parade Isabelle made her way to the front row of spectators and looked at the shoes of the Klansmen as they marched by, dressed in white robes and peaked caps with holes cut for the eyes.

When she saw the shoe with the "X," she shouted, "Daddy, there goes my uncle!" This public disclosure was very embarrassing to the uncle.

The prominence of the KKK in Decatur probably peaked when the robed Klansmen entered the Baptist church that Sunday evening; the organization's prestige and influence declined slowly theraftter.

The decline was gradual, however, and the Klan remained a power in Wise County for several years. On October 26, 1923, the *Wise County Messenger* displayed an advertisement with the following invitation:

KKK JUBILEE
Big Time Refreshments
Alvord, Monday Night, Oct., 29
All Klansmen Welcome

The influence of the Klan was a force in politics, and some members were elected to local and state offices as well as to the

Congress and Senate of the United States. In Texas, however, the KKK did not succeed in electing a governor; its candidate was defeated by Miriam A. Ferguson in 1924 and by Dan Moody, who ran on an anti-Klan platform, in 1926.

The national membership of the Klan was said to be four million in 1924. A year later in 1925 a forty-thousand-man parade of robed klansmen on Pennsylvania Avenue in Washington indicated, by its smart marching, the World War I military experience of many of its members.

The KKK flourished a few years in the South after the Civil War, appeared again during World War I, and thrived for a few years afterward. It reappeared after World War II but did not regain its strength of the 1920's. The present version of the Klan is said to have a rule against wearing masks in public.

As contrasted with the vacillating membership of the Klan, the older secret orders, credited with sponsoring a high order of conduct, were long an important part of community life in Decatur. Even so, a cynical young man, after initiation into such an order, claimed he had had to promise he would not seduce the wife or daughter of another member.

Dad belonged to the Masonic Lodge, Knights of Pythias, and Odd Fellows, secret orders said to sponsor high standards of ethical conduct. Children's homes and hospitals were visible evidence of public service provided by some orders.

Dad, having a low opinion of ostentation, did not see eye to eye with Masonic brothers who were also Shriners. He just did not like to see grown men running around in the business district wearing red fezzes. When he entered the oil business, Dad became inactive in secret orders.

There used to be a yarn that a man had to "ride the goat" when he was initiated into the Masonic Lodge. Dad mentioned that alleged part of the initiation several times to Henry and me, and we wondered how a grown man could possibly ride one. One afternoon when we were ten or eleven years old we were in his office, which was near the Masonic Building on the northwest corner of the courthouse square. Dad decided to play a little practical joke on us and asked us to come upstairs with him to see the goat.

We followed him up the wood stairway and were several feet behind him when he went through an impressive door into the meeting room. As he entered, he let out a loud *ba-a-a*. We were excited about the goat and rushed into the room.

Well, the Ladies of the Eastern Star were in session. One woman sat in a chair that looked like a throne at the east end of the room, and the others sat in chairs around the sides of the room next to the walls. Dad, shocked, started bowing, backing, and apologizing until we were in the hall again with the door to the meeting room closed. And that is what we learned about how the Masons ride the goat.

The selling of life insurance was an important objective of some secret orders. The Praetorian Building at 1607 Main, Dallas, is occupied by the Praetorian Mutual Life Insurance Company. The building and the company are said to have developed from the Praetorian Guards, a secret order that had chapters in many small North Texas towns in the past. I have been told that members had fancy uniforms to wear at their lodge meetings.

The Woodmen of the World obviously managed to sell many tombstones to mark the graves of deceased brothers.

Except for my induction into a college fraternity, I am qualified to write about secret organizations only from the viewpoint of an outsider. Such organizations, however, must involve smaller percentages of the population now than in the early decades of this century. Many lodge buildings in small towns are now in a state of disrepair, whereas they used to be among the best-maintained buildings. Circumstances have changed; television, service clubs, and night sports now make extensive demands on time.

10

Health Care and Funerals

What! Know ye not that your body is the temple of the Holy Ghost. . . .

I Corinthians 6:16

Great progress has been made in preventive medicine in recent years, but the idea of prevention is not new. In the first decades of this century some children went to school wearing smelly bags of asafetida, defined as "the fetid gum resin of various oriental plants." A little bag of the stuff was suspended from a string worn around the neck like a necklace. The asafetida may have kept some wearers from becoming ill by discouraging other children from coming near.

An ailment fairly common among boys at school was itch, commonly called the "seven-year itch." The affliction was prevalent during cold weather, when skin between fingers tended to harden and crack. A friend from another part of the state later told me that itch disappeared in his neighborhood with the introduction of indoor plumbing.

Patent medicines, highly advertised in weekly newspapers at the beginning of this century, were widely used before the U.S. Food and Drug Administration restricted the use of opiates in such remedies. The *Decatur News* in its issues dated September 7, 14, and 21, 1900, advertised nineteen patent medicines, most of which were advertised in all three issues. Those advertised included Mitchell's Eye Salve, Dr. Pierce's Favorite Prescription ("Makes Weak Women Strong and Sick Women Well"), Carter's Little Liver Pills, Piso's Cure for Consumption, Chillfuge, J & C Maguire's Extract, Plantation Chill Cure, SSS, Dr. Tabler's Buckeye Pile Cure, Ely's Cream Balm, Scott's Emulsion, McElree's Wine of Cardui, Lydia E. Pinkham's Vegetable Compound, Certain Chill Cure, Castoria, Tutt's Liver Pills, Teethina, Toe-Gum, and Thompson's Eye Water. Favorites at our house were Castoria, Syrup of Figs, and Syrup of Pepsin.

Although sex was surrounded by many taboos in Wise County at the beginning of this century, the language used by the old-timers was surprisingly frank on the subject. Their frankness tolerated such patent-medicine advertisements in the *Decatur News* as the following on October 27, 1898: "Mrs. Pinkham talks about ovaritis: Ovaritis or inflammation of the ovaries may result from sudden stopping of the monthly flow, from inflammation of the womb and many other causes." This advertisement ran on April 25, 1902: "A pastor's wife cured of pelvic catarrh . . . cured by Peruna." The statement about pelvic catarrh, an ailment that must have been conjured up by an advertisement agency, sounded impressive.

Other "medicine" was bought by many local citizens at medicine shows where pretty girls or magicians did their acts to attract crowds. When the crowd gathered, a forceful and clever salesman sold bottles of liquid, said by skeptics to contain a high percentage of alcohol, guaranteed to cure everything from catarrh to diarrhea. The bottles often sold for a dollar each.

Castor oil was one of the favorite home remedies. The foul-tasting, heavy oil was hard to swallow. Parents were resourceful at thinking up ways to get their children to take the stuff. They often mixed it with orange juice, only to spoil a child's taste for oranges. When they mixed it with coffee, root beer, and other things, the castor oil maintained its identity. As a last resort, parents sometimes held a child's nose shut until he opened his mouth for air and then plopped a tablespoon of the repulsive concoction into his mouth. Through all this agony, nobody questioned the effectiveness of castor oil as a remedy, sometimes an explosive one, for constipation.

When Henry Will was about ten years old, we spent the night at Uncle John Chitwood's house near Grandmother's farm in Haskell County. Henry became ill, and Uncle John made him take half a cup of castor oil. If Henry had been developing appendicitis, the dose might have killed him.

Some remedies were helpful, even as placebos can be helpful today, while others had little effect. Mustard plasters surely stimulated superficial circulation. Coal oil (kerosene) must have killed many bacteria when a wounded foot was soaked in it but was unlikely to kill them in a deep puncture wound.

Dad, troubled with an acid stomach, occasionally mixed baking soda with vinegar and drank the concoction while it was bubbling and foaming. If he failed to use enough soda to more than neutralize the vinegar, his stomach fluids must have become more acid than before.

A favorite cough remedy used by Uncle Newt Barton was a mixture of equal parts whiskey, honey, and glycerine. His children said the mixture was effective.

When a person became really ill and the patent medicines and home remedies did not help, the family asked a doctor to make a house call. Small towns then had no emergency rooms and no hospitals. Sick people either recovered or died at home, except for an occasional individual rich enough to go to Fort Worth for hospitalization.

Most country doctors early in this century had a standard of living comparable to that of other middle class people of their community —often not very impressive. Dr. Arthur Gentry, who married Mama's oldest sister Eureka, and Dr. Joe Gose, who was Mama's uncle, practiced medicine together in Wise County for years. Then they moved to Haskell, where they stayed for the remainder of their professional careers.

They were sometimes paid a calf for delivering a baby, and Dr. Gentry's barnyard often held a calf. Aunt Eureka frequently sewed for other women to earn money to help with household expenses.

Sympathy and consolation were important qualities of our doctors, many of whom received their training in the last decades of the 1800's, went to medical school only about two years, and started their practice without internship. Many made up in service what they lacked in training, making house calls at any time of day or night. Furthermore, many lived and practiced in towns that do not have doctors today. Dr. Ingram and Dr. Petty devoted their careers to taking care of the sick and delivering babies in Wise County.

When a member of our family became ill, which happened rarely, Dr. Ingram made a house call, took temperature, listened to the heart, examined the eyes, looked at the tongue and throat, and said something reassuring. He then sat at a table, opened his black bag (which contained a number of small bottles), and mixed powders on a little slab of marble, using a knife that had a long blade with a straight cutting edge. He folded the powders into little pieces of waxed paper and left instructions as to how often to give the powders to the patient. I have long suspected that the powders were aspirin or calomel. Sometimes he sent out a prescription in a bottle. His concern for his patients was genuine, and his willingness to go to a lot of trouble to minister to them was never questioned. Dr. Petty was equally dedicated and helpful.

When I was six years old, my tonsils were infected. Removal was then generally considered to be the proper treatment, even though there was no hospital closer than Fort Worth.

Dad, after consultation with Dr. Ingram, arranged to have my tonsils removed. We went to the doctor's office, where the big patient's chair was laid back as a flat operating table. Other fixtures were pushed back so there was room to walk around the table. Because of the seriousness of the procedure, Dr. Petty, the town's other family doctor, was standing by as a consultant.

Dad laid me on the table, and the doctor put a thing over my face that was something like a lightweight catcher's mask, except that it was covered with a white cloth.

The doctor asked, "Can you count?"

"Yes, sir."

"How high can you count?" he asked, as he poured some ether on the cloth.

"One, two, three, four, five," and I stopped when I breathed some of the smothering, overpowering ether. After starting over several times, I lost consciousness.

Dad, who stayed in the office and observed the surgery, later said that the doctor had trouble getting my tonsils out and finally used his fingers to help remove them.

The next thing I remember is that I was sitting on Dad's lap in Dr. Ingram's Model T Ford coupe as the doctor drove us home. My throat hurt.

Some people were vaccinated for smallpox, but vaccinations and inoculations were rare; some people were vaccinated for the first time when they entered military service or went away to college.

Victims of tuberculosis were often told to go west and work outdoors in the fresh air. This medical advice often meant going to a ranch and roughing it, which sometimes turned out to be the equivalent of a death sentence. The treatment today requires rest. The prevalence of tuberculosis and mortality from it were greater then than now.

The son of one of our Methodist preachers enjoyed telling yarns and had a kinsman to illustrate almost any situation. He told us a story about an uncle who was an old-time doctor in Bastrop. For years the doctor made house calls and delivered babies for a family that lived in the river bottom about five miles from town. He never sent the family a bill because he knew they had no money. After some years of this care, the man of the family inherited a substantial amount of money, and the doctor sent a bill for his previous years of service. The patient was outraged and refused to make any payment on the bill. After failing in a number of efforts to collect, the doctor saw his patient in town wearing a new suit. The doctor knocked him down and then jumped on him and slapped him around a little.

The doctor had his bill ready and marked "paid in full," and he pinned the bill on the man's new coat. After checking the bill to be sure it was firmly attached, the doctor got up, dusted off his clothes, and walked away with a little smile on his face.

The preacher's son told us another yarn, this one about an uncle who was a doctor in Llano. One night he received a call to come to the home of an old bachelor rancher who was known to be very tight with his money. The rancher was moaning in the middle of his bed and rocking back and forth on his hands and knees. The doctor diagnosed the problem as a kidney stone and gave the patient a hypodermic injection to ease his pain and relax the muscles. Then the doctor sat in a chair beside the bed and talked calmly to the rancher about the weather, the price of cattle, the feed crop, and the like. The old rancher gradually relaxed and finally stretched out in bed.

The preacher's boy quoted his uncle as saying, "I could just see that stingy old codger's mind working; he was thinking, 'That sonabitch is charging me for just sitting there and talking to me.' "

The old rancher said, "Godammit, Doc, I didn't invite you here for a social visit!"

"I knew then he was completely relaxed, felt no pain, and had a fair chance of passing the stone."

Dental techniques were more primitive in the early 1920's than now. Our family dentist was Dr. Payne, a conscientious man who put a dozen or more fillings in my teeth when I was about twelve years old. Possibly my habit of eating sugar between meals had something to do with my need for dental services.

Dr. Payne used a foot treadle to power the drill and was expert at standing on his left foot while working the treadle with his right foot. The drills were kept in a little round wood container with the burrs up. After Dr. Payne replaced a used drill, he turned the container by pulling the burrs with his forefinger until he found the one he wanted. Once he was drilling one of my teeth when the belt slipped and the burr jammed. It was a challenge to Dr. Payne to free the drill again.

When the doctor made amalgam for a filling, he placed powdered silver in his left hand and shook some mercury on it from a small black container that had a little hole at the top like a pepper shaker. Then he rubbed mercury into the silver with his right forefinger and filled cavities with the resulting amalgam. I still have some small fillings he made by hammering gold foil into tiny cavities. All this was done without a shot to ease pain.

When a patient died, our doctors in Decatur consoled the family and went to the funeral, a service often neglected by our highly specialized medical profession today.

Some people think it is a mistake to take young children to funerals, but no such feeling prevailed in Decatur when my brother and I were boys. Some of our early memories are of funerals.

Around the time of World War I the funeral customs in rural areas were different from those in cities like Waco. Hardware and furniture stores advertised coffins rather than general undertaking services. When Great-aunt Cora Sellers died in 1915, the funeral service was held at her home. A crowd of friends and neighbors gathered in the house and front yard, and the preacher conducted the service there. Her body was put in the coffin at home before the service. After the service, the casket was placed in a fancy horse-drawn hearse, which led the procession of buggies and a few cars along the dusty road to Oaklawn Cemetery north of town. Shortly after the graveside service, some of the men picked up shovels and energetically started filling the grave. It is hard to forget the finality of the "thunk" heard when the first shovel of dirt and clods hit the casket.

When Great-aunt Martha Harding died in 1919, men removed the coffin from her house by passing it out through a window because they could not maneuver it around through the hall without disturbing her body. Otherwise, her service was much like Aunt Cora's.

Most of the funerals I remember were for older family members, but death was not confined to the elderly. On July 24, 1921, Uncle Labry E. Ballard, Jr., only twenty-six years old and Aunt Irene's husband, was killed in an accident on the Ballard ranch in Haskell County.

Paint Creek, on the Ballard ranch, was perhaps the best fishing place in the county. Where the clear stream flowed through a canyon, large channel catfish as well as smaller varieties lurked in deep pools. Uncle Labry's sister organized an overnight fishing party at Paint Creek, and the family arranged for a cook, equipped with a chuck wagon, to meet the group and prepare the food. The chuck wagon, pulled by a pair of mules, was supplied with plenty of food, Dutch ovens, skillets, and other utensils. The cook hobbled the mules, hoping they would not wander far from camp.

In the meantime, Aunt Irene, then seven months pregnant, and her daughter Helen, almost a year and a half old, were in another part of the county visiting Aunt Irene's mother (Grandma, to Henry and me) and her brothers at the Perrin farm.

After a successful outing and fish fry, the guests departed, leaving the cook to find the mules, get them back to the chuck wagon, and harness them.

Uncle Labry rode his horse to the Paint Creek fishing area to visit the guests, only to find that they had gone and the cook was unable to find his mules. Uncle Labry found the mules, still hobbled, a surprising distance from the campsite. He roped one of them and managed to get the other end of his lariat around the neck of the second mule. He then tied a simple knot about halfway between the end of the doubled lariat and the mules, intending to keep the animals close together after mounting his horse to lead them back to the chuck wagon. When Uncle Labry removed the hobbles, the mules bolted. The lariat tangled around him, and the mules dragged him through mesquite brush and over hard soil and rocks.

His body was found two days later, and Dr. Gentry said he had died only a short time previously. The grass and weeds indicated that he had crawled around a mesquite tree seeking protection from the hot July sun in the sparse shade of the tree.

When word of Uncle Labry's death was phoned to the Perrin farm, the family hurriedly prepared for the ten-mile drive to town. Uncle Carl, feeling deeply the emotion of the situation, tried to pick up little Helen. She, knowing that she was going to town and not understanding death, said, "No, I'm going to see my daddy," and turned away. When she saw her daddy, he was in a coffin.

In accordance with the custom in small Texas towns in the early 1920's, the funeral was conducted in the Ballard home in Haskell. The families, relatives, and neighbors were in the house during the service, and many friends were on the front porch and in the front yard.

Labry E. Ballard, III, was born on September 27, 1921; his father's funeral was probably the saddest I have ever attended.

Within a few years church funerals became the custom, and the family occupied pews at the front, with the open coffin placed between the first pew and the pulpit. Most friends and neighbors walked down the aisle and took a last look at the deceased before taking their seats in the congregation.

Some families bore their grief stoically, and others wept unrestrainedly, especially during the singing of such songs as "Shall We Gather at the River," "Abide with Me," "Rock of Ages," "God Be with You," and "The Old Rugged Cross."

The preacher quoted scripture, prayed, said kind words about the deceased and the mercy of God, and comforted the family. Some departed members of the congregation rated first-class eulogies.

The grandsons and husbands of granddaughters were pallbearers at Grandma Barton's funeral at Red Oak, Texas, in 1926. It looked natural for her to hold a Bible in her hands, because she had read it every day.

The Masonic Lodge, often involved in funerals for men, put on an impressive performance. Several Masons, wearing their hats, stood in line, with their leader to one side. The leader always had a strong, resonant voice, and the men wore little white aprons said to be made of lamb's skin. The leader recited a liturgy. When he referred to the Deity, all the men lifted their hats from their heads and returned them in unison. At certain points the men in the line said, "So mote it be." When the ceremony was over, there was a feeling that the departed brother was well buried.

One day the preacher's boy, who lived across the street, told us a story that his father had heard about a funeral conducted by a preacher of a fundamentalist denomination in a small town in West Texas. The deceased, although not a religious man, belonged to a church with his family, but he had the misfortune of being killed in a drunken brawl resulting from a misunderstanding in a poker game.

The funeral was conducted in a little church with the coffin open. The family, upset by the tragic and untimely death, sat in the pews nearest the casket.

The family got no consolation from the preacher, who said, "Our friend, John Doe, was killed in a drunken brawl and has gone to hell! If some of you folks out there don't repent, you'll burn in hell, too!" He then preached a sermon calling on sinners to repent.

The preacher's boy concluded the story by quoting his father: "That family needs consolation and help, but I don't know how to give it to them."

11

Gun Culture

A well regulated militia, being necessary to the security of a free state, the right of the people to keep and bear arms, shall not be infringed.
CONSTITUTION OF THE UNITED STATES

Gun culture is part of our heritage in the South. Two reasons are, first, that we are removed from a rural environment and pioneer conditions by only a few generations, and, second, that the period of reconstruction after the Civil War lasted until 1877, when President Hayes ordered the last of the occupation troops out of the defeated South. As pointed out in Otis A. Singletary's *Negro Militia and Reconstruction*, the South armed itself during its occupation. Rifle clubs, saber clubs, and other military-type organizations were numerous and active, with many members being Confederate veterans.

Dad was born in 1876, when the South was emerging from reconstruction with its economy deeply depressed under the dual burden of financing its recovery while paying the cost of its occupation. Dad's family lived in the hill country of Bedford and Coffee counties, about seventy miles south of Nashville, Tennessee. The parents and five children worked long and hard to glean a subsistence from a small hillside farm.

The farmers were armed and used their guns to protect their homes and to shoot wild game to supplement their limited diet. Dad once said he was sure he had killed a wagon load of squirrels with the family's double-barrel muzzle-loader shotgun.

Dad was a gun enthusiast throughout his life, and I remember having the following guns in our home: the muzzle-loading shotgun he used as a boy in Tennessee, a .30-.30 Marlin carbine, an automatic 12-gauge shotgun, a .32 caliber Colt automatic, a .22 caliber Winchester pump rifle, a .32 caliber Smith & Wesson six-shooter, a .38 caliber Smith & Wesson special revolver, and a .45 caliber Smith & Wesson revolver (model 1917).

All except the muzzle loader, an heirloom, were kept loaded. My brother and I knew from a tender age that all guns were loaded, and we did not play with them. (I have not used the loaded gun procedure with my children but have taught them to treat every gun as loaded.)

When I was five or six years old, I noticed that the door from our kitchen to the back porch had several spots that looked different from the rest of the door. The spots, little and round, were filled with putty that was stained and varnished. Eventually I learned why the spots were there. Shortly after we moved into our new house, probably late in 1911, Dad heard crashing and thumping noises on the back porch late one night. Thinking someone was trying to break into our home, he shouted a warning and then, when he heard no reply from the presumed assailant, fired several times through the door. He then opened the door and found that a dog had broken through the screen and was jerking a ham out of the evaporative cooler in which we kept our milk, butter, and meat. The episode had a happy ending, because Dad protected his home and the dog escaped. Dad defended our home strongly against all threats.

Young boys who believe in Santa Claus are filled with excitement and anticipation when they wake up on Christmas morning. For us it was different in 1918. Henry and I woke up early but sensed that something was wrong. We looked from our folding bed across the room to the bed where Dad and Mama slept and saw Dad lying on his back with a big bandage around his neck. The toys had not been put out, and we almost forgot about Christmas in our concern for Dad.

We soon found out what had happened and later heard the story read aloud from the two local weekly newspapers. On Christmas Eve night, Dad heard men shouting at the house across the street. Knowing that the husband was out of town and that only a woman and her daughter were at home, Dad ran across the street and recognized three young men who were recent students in Decatur High School.

One was beating on the front door of the house trying to get in and was stabbing the door facing with his knife. The other two young men were standing to one side, and all three were obviously drunk. Dad ordered the young man away from the door by name and pulled him away when there was no proper response. Dad got the young man down on the ground and slapped him into some kind of soberness. In the melee, the young man cut Dad's throat with the small blade of his knife, the slash coming within a quarter of an inch of Dad's jugular. Fortunately, the young man had broken the big blade while stabbing on the door facing.

The reason this knifing story is in the discussion on gun culture is that Dad had a revolver in his pocket but would not use it because he knew the young man. The young man's father later said that he would not have held it against Dad if he had used his pistol.

Mama, Henry, and I often visited Grandpa and Grandma Perrin at their farm near Sycamore in northeast Wise County. Their firearms included a shotgun and a .22 rifle. We were on a visit in 1917 when Grandma ran into the house, grabbed the shotgun, and shot at a chicken hawk that was trying to get her baby chicks. The blast saved the chicks by scaring the hawk away.

In the summer of 1918 we visited Grandma Barton, Aunt Sallie (Dad's sister), and various cousins at Red Oak, a small farm community about twenty miles south of Dallas. Uncle Newt Lowrance had a fine farm on the rich blackland prairie near town, and his impressive house with a long front porch was in a grove of trees, including several red oaks.

The family and guests gathered for dinner (at noon) at the Lowrance home on a warm, humid Sunday, after attending a lengthy service at the Methodist church. After a large meal, the men sat in chairs on the porch and talked about the war, the weather, the crops, and the sermon. The women, after washing and drying the dishes, joined the men on the porch and talked among themselves. The only sounds other than the quiet conversations were the clucking of the hens and the shouts of the children as they ran and played around the house.

The conversation had slowed, and some of the men had begun to appear drowsy when one of them suggested, "Let's have a little target practice." Without further discussion, the men went variously into the house or to their automobiles and returned with revolvers.

Cousin Willie, about twelve years old, ran into the house and came out with a single-shot .22 rifle, one of the safest of guns. My brother, Henry Will, about seven years old, attempted to load Willie's rifle and got the shell in front of the extractor. When he closed the bolt, the extractor compressed the rim of the shell and fired a round into the front-porch steps. Nobody appeared very upset by this accident. Uncle Newt attached a target to one of the trees, and the Sunday afternoon was neither quiet nor drowsy while the target practice continued about an hour.

From 1916 to 1926 Dad was in the oil business in the Wichita Falls area while maintaining the family residence eighty miles away at Decatur. His long hours in oil promotion and exploration were supplemented by travel to Decatur over poor roads. He always carried a handgun on those trips, usually his .32 caliber Smith & Wesson revolver. When Henry and I were twelve or thirteen years old, we traveled to Wichita Falls with Dad in his new Chandler touring car, accompanied by another car of relatives and business associates. The road was rough and dusty, and we stopped in the ranch country of Clay County for a little rest.

The men broke the tedium of travel by getting out their revolvers and firing a few rounds at fence posts. Henry and I were honored because Dad invited us to fire a round or two. After receiving specific instructions, I drew a steady bead on a post and squeezed the trigger. Although I had heard guns fired many times previously, I was not prepared for the shock of the explosion so close to my ears. I was successful, since I hit the post, but for the first time I heard a ringing in my ears. I still hear a ringing and believe my ears have been ringing to some extent since I first fired a six-shooter at a fence post.

Dad's widowed sister, Aunt Sallie Davis, lived at Red Oak with her five children and Grandma Barton. One night in 1924, a man came into Aunt Sallie's house late at night, while the family was asleep. Aunt Sallie awakened and quietly got out of bed with a flashlight in her left hand and a revolver in her right hand. She flashed the light toward the intruder in such a way that some of the light revealed the revolver pointed toward him, and he made a quick exit.

When Henry and I were twelve and fourteen, Dad bought each of us a double-barrel 12-gauge shotgun of the best quality. When I fired mine the first time, I rested the barrel on top of a fence post and aimed at a dove in a tree a considerable distance away. The post was high for me, and I stood on my toes as the gun fired. The kick knocked me back on my seat, and that is how I learned the importance of good footing when firing a gun.

A momentary lapse of attention in the use of firearms can be deadly. In 1926 two of my cousins were hunting. Julian Perrin was walking through some brush ahead of Perrin Gentry, who was carrying a little single-shot 410 shotgun. Gentry carelessly cocked his gun, and either his finger or a twig touched the trigger. The gun fired, and the pellets went between Julian's legs. (Julian's luck stayed with him, because he later logged over three hundred days of World War II combat with a mortar outfit in Europe without being wounded.) Julian's close call impressed on me Dad's instruction, "Never get in front of a man who has a gun."

When Henry and I were ten or twelve years old, the Roach brothers visited us one afternoon. When we walked by the bed where Dad and Mama slept, I turned Dad's pillow back, exposing a loaded revolver. Nobody touched it, but I still feel uncomfortable when I think about the possibilities.

My generation had no idea that anything could be wrong in owning a gun. The thought that the government might even consider prohibition of ownership was totally foreign.

12

World War I

The division of Europe into two armed camps took place by slow stages over a period of forty years.

BRIGADIER GENERAL S. L. A. MARSHALL

When World War I was being waged in the fields and trenches of France in 1914 and 1915, the people of Wise County felt secure from the distant battles. At that time the United States was having trouble with its neighbor Mexico. Perhaps some citizens of the county had misgivings when the *Decatur News* announced in a headline on April 17, 1914, "Entire Atlantic Fleet to Tampico," but fears were not widespread.

The war came closer in 1915 when the *Lusitania*, under the flag of Great Britain, was sunk on May 7 by a German submarine near the British coast and carried 128 Americans to their deaths. The *Decatur News* reported the tragedy in a headline saying, "Lusitania Torpedoed; 1200 Perish."

News of the sinking added to a feeling of resentment beginning to build up against Americans of German heritage. This emotion of prejudice grew during 1916 and into 1917, when on February 4 the *Fort Worth Star-Telegram* featured a headline saying, "Attempt to Sink U.S. Torpedo Boat by Sailor, Said to Be of German Parentage."

The Americans of German descent suffered a more severe blow on March 1 of that year, when the *Star-Telegram* ran the following headline: "Zimmerman Letter Revealing Mexican Plot." The story disclosed quotations from a message sent from the German foreign secretary to the German ambassador to Mexico. The message included the following threat to Texas: ". . . and it is to be understood that Mexico is to recover the lost territory in New Mexico, Texas and Arizona."

Headlines of the *Star-Telegram* from January 23, 1917, to April 28, 1917, are a record of the rising emotion of war and the commitment to combat in Wise County and the West Texas area.

Jan. 23 Orders Given to Withdraw Outposts of Mexico Force
Feb. 3 Wilson Says Break with Germany Only Choice Left
Feb. 4 Sinking American Ship Brings U.S. Nearer War
Feb. 8 War Only Question of Time
Sinking of *California* Is Not Ground Enough But Overt Act Expected Soon
Feb. 14 U-Boat Sinks U.S. Vessel
Mar. 3 Berlin Defends Sending Note to Stir up Mexico
Mar. 27 Texans Stay in Service
Apr. 1 War Department Is Ready to Take up Organization of Million Men
Apr. 2 Lodge [Senator from Massachusetts] Knocks Down Pacifist in Fist Fight
Apr. 3 Texas Guardsmen Are Ordered to Fort Sam Houston
Apr. 6 Wilson Signs War Decree
Apr. 12 U.S. Seeks 500,000 Volunteers
Apr. 23 Conscription Fight Begun
Apr. 28 Vote Favors Conscription

When war was declared, the people of Wise County were part of an innocent grass-roots surge of patriotism that moved across the country. We soon heard drill orders shouted on the County Fairground east of the railroad tracks. Decatur's National Guard company was being drilled. The company shipped out and was an effective combat infantry outfit in Europe under the command of Captain Steve Lillard.

Shortly before Decatur's young men left for war, Lawrence Melton came to our house to visit Dad, possibly to say goodbye to his former teacher and superintendent. I looked in the parlor and saw Melton in his impressive new uniform and heard him say, "When I hear the 'Star-Spangled Banner,' I stand at attention and salute."

I then made a nuisance of myself by begging Dad to play the song on our new Edison. My requests were ignored.

With the departure of our National Guard company, local feelings against Americans of German heritage became more intense, and we heard stories of yellow paint being thrown on houses occupied by people with German names. Uncomplimentary remarks were made about the fine old gentleman who operated the town's best little restaurant. A few critical comments were even made about Franz Gruen, the town's baker and confectioner from Austria. These uncomplimentary statements were made though Gruen went to the authorities and volunteered, saying, "Don't send these boys to war; they haven't been trained—so just send me." He had received compulsory military training in the old country but was loyal to his adopted homeland.

The prejudice against things German, combined with patriotic spirit, was felt even by young children. An incident in another Texas county was typical. Hallie, my wife, was six years old in the spring of 1918 when she visited a girl who was about a year younger. Her friend's *oma* ("grandmother") was talking with an elderly cousin, and their conversation was all in German. The little girls, outraged by this treasonous conduct, shouldered little American flags and marched through the parlor where the old ladies were talking. As they marched, the girls sang "America" loudly. The miniature patriotic parade continued intermittently throughout the afternoon until the little friend's mother returned and stopped it. In the meantime, the old ladies continued their conversation.

When the government wanted peach seeds to use in making the right kind of charcoal for gas masks, the boys of the neighborhood looked under peach trees for seeds left from overripe or wormy peaches that had fallen off and rotted. We gathered enough seeds to fill a large box. We also collected tinfoil and toothpaste tubes but never heard how or whether these items were used.

We had a garden southwest of the house. The only perennial was a big sage plant near the gate. The sage was used for seasoning, especially in sausage. During World War I, our garden became a victory garden and was worked with special fervor. Henry and I worked harder because we thought we were helping win the war.

The boys in the neighborhood played war games and used ingenuity in devising weapons. We made a cannon from a two-foot length of two-inch pipe mounted on a sturdy box. We put a piece of half-inch pipe about a foot long in the large pipe, leaving about an inch of the small pipe sticking out of the breech. We hit the protruding end of the small pipe with a heavy hammer, transforming it into a projectile that went four or five feet. Fortunately, the weapons caused no casualties because nobody wanted to play German when it was used.

The government sponsored big drives to sell Liberty Bonds, and the children went to rallies on the courthouse square and wanted to buy bonds. The government, anticipating this response, sold War Savings Stamps to children and others who could not afford bonds. Many adults bought bonds "to help our soldier boys."

The United States entered the war about fourteen years after the Wright brothers made their first flight, and airplanes were still new and exciting. Once when a plane flew over Decatur, the teachers interrupted classes long enough for us to file outside and look.

More than half the 116,516 soldiers and sailors who died during the war were victims of disease. In approximately three months (September through November, 1918), influenza and pneumonia killed some 42,500 servicemen, and over 621,000 were infected with diseases that year. Precise diagnosis as to influenza or pneumonia, which sometimes occurred simultaneously, was difficult and often impossible because of the volume of illness and relative shortage of doctors. Military effectiveness was impaired by the large number of deaths and the temporary disability of those who survived.

The epidemic also afflicted a large proportion of the civilian population. In a survey of selected cities and towns, the U.S. Public Health Service estimated that 28 percent of the people had contracted influenza.

Henry Will and I were six and seven years old when Dad, with a high fever, returned home with influenza he had caught in the oil fields around Wichita Falls. Mama contracted the virus, and both were sick at the same time. The neighbors would not come into the house, and the doctor wore a cloth over his nose and mouth when he came.

Henry and I nursed our parents and thought we did a great job. We carried glasses of water and made toast in the oven of the gas range in the kitchen. Our toast was a major production, being about equal parts of butter and bread. Dad and Mom recovered in spite of our nursing care.

The joy in Decatur on Armistice Day, November 11, 1918, must have been comparable to that throughout the United States. People laughed, shouted, and paraded around the courthouse square. Mr. Cohen, our Jewish junk man, sat on the right front fender of a decorated parade car, happily beating the bottom of a small washtub.

The Armistice celebration sounded more like a battle than the happy end of war. Part of the festivities involved the firing of anvils on the square. An anvil was placed upside down, exposing a cavity in its base. The cavity was filled with black gunpowder, and a little trail was poured from the cavity to the edge of the anvil. Then a second anvil was set over the cavity. The trail of powder was ignited with the red-hot end of a long iron rod. The loud explosion produced a strong concussion. We almost had a celebration casualty to add to our war casualties. An eager anvil shooter poured some powder too quickly after a blast, and a spark was still in the anvil. The powder flashed back. Fortunately, the fellow lost only his shirt and received only superficial burns.

I remember the funerals of Corporal Monte E. Dunaway and Corporal Lloyd Smith, two of our Wise County soldiers. There were other such funerals, but those two made a vivid impression. Both were killed in battle, Lloyd Smith after being wounded in the shoulder and ordered to the rear for treatment. But he was over there to fight and, refusing to go to the rear, he went on into battle. The funerals were after the war was over, and Captain Lillard and many of their buddies were present. The services were with military honors, and I was greatly impressed when the rifles were fired over the graves.

When our soldiers came home, they were reluctant to talk about their experiences. Or perhaps they talked to each other but did not talk much to people who had not been "over there." Gradually, however, stories began to trickle out from families and friends of veterans from Decatur and other Texas towns. The following stories were told by men who were veterans of World War I and who served with different outfits. A few Wise County boys were probably in each outfit.

One story, related to me by a fellow drilling rig worker, happened to an infantry company after it disembarked at Brest. The company marched in formation along a street where several sidewalk urinals caught the attention of the men. The captain, a gentleman of Irish heritage, noticed that his men had diverted their attention from the cadence of the march to the urinals and shouted, "Company, halt!" He ordered the soldiers to relieve themselves where they stood, and the troops obeyed the command to the best of their abilities. A few soldiers in the front rank heard the captain mutter, "These French ain't going to get ahead of us on anything!"

Another story, told by an officer who was a graduate of the U.S. Military Academy, was about two new battalions on their way to the front. The last night before the men were to go into the line, the battalions bivouacked on a large hillside. The men were ordered to put up pup tents. The officer telling the story ordered his men to strike no matches and make no fires whatsoever. The other commander, who had come to fight and not to read machine-duplicated instructions, issued a candle to each of his men. He passed the word that the last night before battle would be a good time to write letters home. After dark his battalion was a beautiful sight, each little tent with a lighted candle in it.

German planes flew over the illuminated battalion several times while the soldiers were writing letters. The pilots, obviously studying the situation, finally flew away without dropping bombs, having concluded that the Allies had set up a trap to get them to waste bombs on empty tents.

A friend who had been an ambulance driver sometimes yelled and woke up at night dreaming about something that happened to him in the war. The memory that haunted him happened when he was driving slowly along a muddy, slick road at night without lights and saw a uniformed body lying on the narrow road. He steered the ambulance, which was nothing more than a panel truck, toward the ditch in order to miss the body. The sergeant sitting beside him yelled "You're going to get us stuck; godammit, run over him!" The former ambulance driver still wondered whether the body had been dead or alive.

A Marine colonel I new in World War II told a story about some action he had seen in World War I in the heavy fighting at Belleau Wood. The story concerned a sergeant he had known well. At one time during the battle the sergeant was in a shell hole in an exposed area with three men and a machine gun. He was ordered to hold the right end of a meadow while the remainder of his company, positioned behind trees and boulders, countered the charge of three German companies with aimed rifle fire.

The enemy mortar and machine-gun fire was intense when the Germans started their charge, and the three men in the hole with the sergeant started scrambling out toward the rear. At that point the sergeant jumped out, exposing himself to the enemy fire, and shouted, "I'll kill every sonabitch that comes out of that hole. Stay in there and fight, godammit."

The sergeant miraculously survived the enemy bullets, and somehow the machine gunners held their point while the German charge crumpled under the deadly aim of the Marine marksmen.

The lieutenant commended the sergeant for his bravery and said he would recommend a high award for valor. The sergeant was pleased with the prospect, especially when his captain said, "I know a soldier who got the Congressional Medal of Honor for doing something no braver than what you did." After hearing that, the sergeant hoped he might get the coveted Navy Cross.

A few weeks passed, and no award appeared. Finally, the sergeant heard the scuttlebutt that the recommendation for his commendation had been written much like the foregoing account and did not include such expressions as "without regard for his personal safety," "in keeping with the highest traditions of the U.S. Marine Corps," or "above and beyond the call of duty." The sergeant then realized that medals are awarded for cliches as well as for courage in battle.

The young man from Decatur who did receive a high award for valor was from an exceptionally poor and uneducated family. When asked about his bravery, he just smiled and walked away.

13

Tobacco and Corn Whiskey

*And be not drunk . . . wherein is excess; but be
filled with the spirit. . . .*

EPHESIANS 5:18

If Dad told us about his early smoking experience in order to impress
us with the evils of tobacco, he succeeded. Dad smoked a few cigars
during his first year at Winchester Normal College and a few more
on the sly after returning to the family's hillside farm the following
summer.

About a month after his return, his mother found a cigar in his
shirt pocket. Grandpa called Dad into the parlor of their little house,
handed him the cigar and instructed him to smoke it. Dad said, "No,
Pa, I don't want to smoke that cigar in here with you and Ma."

A steely look appeared in the old man's eyes, the kind of look he
sometimes showed when he talked about his battle experiences when
he was Corporal Barton in the Army of Tennessee during the Civil
War. He spoke slowly as he said, "Son, you will smoke that cigar,
here, right now."

Dad sat in a chair by the fireplace, lit the cigar, and smoked it,
while hearing such comments as, "My, don't you think he handles
it nicely?" "See how gracefully he puffs the smoke!" "He hasn't
made a smoke ring yet." "Can you blow smoke out of your nose?"
"Aren't we proud of him!"

Dad said he puffed rapidly, but the cigar seemed to last an hour.
When he finished the cigar, he was through with smoking.

There were almost as many tobacco chewers in Decatur as smokers. It was the custom of most of the gentlemen who sat on the
courthouse steps to move around the building in warm weather to
stay in the shade and in cold weather to stay in the sun. It was also
their custom, with a few exceptions, to chew tobacco, and they

developed impressive skill in the gentle art of spitting. The spitter pursed his lips tightly, thrust his tongue forward quickly, and expelled a bullet-shaped blob of tobacco juice with impressive accuracy. One gentleman was said to be able to hit a housefly on the courthouse steps before it could fly away.

The gentlemen did more than chew tobacco. They discussed major world problems, commented on local and national politics, noticed pretty women, and made occasional observations of a philosophical character.

Smokers were of several types. Many "rolled their own," usually with Bull Durham tobacco sold in little cloth bags with drawstrings at the top. Thin cigarette papers, made in France, were in a little folder attached to the side of the bag. Skillful rollers fashioned cigarettes with just one hand. The more affluent cigarette smokers bought packages of tailor-made ones of the usual brands. In addition, others smoked cigars or pipes, the latter usually stoked with Prince Albert tobacco, which came in a pretty red can made to fit into a shirt pocket. The can had a picture of Prince Albert on the front.

Although we sometimes called cigarettes "coffin nails," there was no general belief that tobacco was harmful. People were beginning to wonder, however; the *Decatur News* printed a story on May 16, 1912, to the effect that a man in Pennsylvania had died from smoking 180,000 cigarettes in ten years. The article moralized that ". . . his life [was] of little value except to help along the cigarette business. . . ."

Although our parents did not smoke, my brother and I, along with other neighborhood kids, experimented with smoking. Henry once tried real cigarettes with the tomboy who played baseball and football with us. When he got sick and she did not, we terminated our experience with tobacco. We continued other smoking experiments, however, trying grapevine, corn silk, coffee, tea, sunflower leaves, morning glory leaves, and Cubebs from the drug store. We concluded that morning glory leaves were the best and sunflower leaves the worst.

Most people in Wise County worked too hard to be concerned with the dearth of economic and social activity that characterized periods between elections, fires, and protracted meetings. Some citizens, however, turned to drink, an addiction frowned on by most of the hardworking, church-going folks.

Family use of alcohol, in the manner of the German communities of Central Texas, was almost unknown in Wise County, where alcohol generally was used by men in the form of corn whiskey and by some women in various patent medicines. The Scotch-Irish types who settled much of North Texas, being pioneers and men of action, tended to become violent when under the influence of alcohol. The drinking of corn whiskey therefore came to be equated with evil, and prohibition flourished in the area even before enactment of the Eighteenth Amendment.

On March 21, 1902, the *Decatur News* reported the results of elections on prohibition in Wise County as follows:

	1902	1900
For prohibition	2,606	2,246
Against prohibition	1,247	1,528

Even though violence and vice, such as fighting or going to the whorehouses in Fort Worth, were widely attributed to alcohol and although the sale of alcohol was made illegal in Decatur long before enactment of the Eighteenth Amendment, a few amiable drunks managed to find adequate supplies.

One such was a clever lawyer, who surprised his prohibitionist friends by responding to a talk made on the courthouse steps by a representative of the liquor industry. The visitor made the point that the citizens should vote to authorize the sale of liquor "because the people are getting all the liquor they want anyway."

At the conclusion of the visitor's talk, the local attorney, who was as well known for his eloquence as his devotion to corn whiskey, stood on the courthouse steps and said, "Now, I'm going to make a speech!"

The visitor started to walk away, and the lawyer said: "Now, you just wait a minute. I listened to you, and you can just listen to me. It's true that crooks like you and me can get all the whiskey we want at the Blind Tigers, but let's think about our good, law-abiding citizens. They won't go into one of those joints, and the prohibition law delivers them from temptation." The unexpected contribution by the well-known imbiber got a big cheer from his surprised prohibitionist friends.

A theological student at Decatur Baptist College decided to talk to the attorney about drinking and his immortal soul. The ambitious young man decided to appeal to the attorney's reason, but found him a bit irrational from the use of alcohol. Nevertheless the theological student launched his effort in the lawyer's office by saying, "You and I have many things in common. We are both good Baptists, and are both lifelong Democrats, and we. . . ."

At that point the attorney cut in to say, "Yes, and we're both smart sonsabitches," thus terminating the interview.

My mother came from a family of dedicated prohibitionists, and the main thing she understood about liquor was that she hated it, as evidenced by her active membership in the Women's Christian Temperance Union, an organization that more appropriately might have been named the Abstinence Union. Dad, on the other hand, came from a Tennessee farm family where a small keg of "Jack Dan'l" sour mash whiskey was available to all. On his own, Dad decided to stop drinking whiskey when he was a young man. He felt strongly, however, that whiskey had important medicinal values, and therefore he sometimes acquired a pint.

It must have been about 1918 that Dad returned from Wichita Falls with a pint of bourbon concealed in his bag. Mama invited several of her family to come to our home for Sunday dinner and asked Dad to freeze the ice cream. He sneaked a slug of whiskey into the freezer, and Mama received many compliments from her family on the ice cream. Some called it the best they had ever eaten. On request, she gave the recipe to several guests, but they were unable to match the delicious flavor.

The medicinal quality of whiskey was sometimes overestimated.

This became clear when the influenza epidemic of 1918 and 1919 revived viciously for a short time early in 1920. In January of that year, Uncle Joe Barton, who had been superintendent of the Decatur Public Schools before Dad assumed that position, became critically ill with influenza and pneumonia at his home in Waco.

Uncle Newt and Aunt Louise Barton became seriously ill with the same ailment at their home in Waxahachie. Uncle Newt, having bought a case of whiskey for medicinal purposes just before the saloons were closed, felt compelled to deliver a bottle to his brother in Waco, in the desperate hope that Uncle Joe's life might be prolonged.

By that time the Volstead Act, enacted in 1919, was in force, and transportation of whiskey for personal use was a felony. Uncle Newt would gladly have risked arrest to deliver the whiskey, but he was too sick to leave home. His first move in solving the problem was to pack a bottle and some clothing in a little grip (handbag).

He explained the situation to Clara, his ten-year-old daughter, and asked her to make the seventy-mile trip to Waco on the interurban (an electric passenger service) and to deliver the handbag to a man who would meet her at the station. Clara felt like a big girl and had no fear about her important mission. A local friend took Clara to the station, bought her a round-trip ticket, found her a seat, put her in care of the conductor, and placed the bag and its illegal contents on the luggage rack above her head.

Clara knew about prohibition but was calm, understanding the crucial nature of her journey, and was not disturbed when a man wearing a badge got on at Hillsboro. The trip took two hours, and the lawmen walked the length of the car several times as it bounced along the rails. Clara stayed quietly in her seat.

A family friend met her at the Waco station, picked up the grip, helped her off the interurban, and bought her a lunch at the station coffee shop. When the friend put her on the interurban for the return to Waxahachie and the car started lurching home, Clara had the feeling of having accomplished an important mission.

In spite of Clara's heroic trip, Uncle Joe, a handsome and husky man, died in a few days. Uncle Newt and Aunt Louise were too sick to go to the funeral but sent their three children (Clara, Ruby Dean, and Ben) to Waco for the funeral. There were so many flowers they could not see the grave.

14

This and That

For there must be precept upon precept . . .
line upon line; here a little and there a little. . . .
ISAIAH 28:10

While lives are changed drastically by traumatic events, our day-to-day happenings, the "this and that" of our lives, usually mold our personalities, attitudes, and ambitions.

On May 16, 1902, the editor and owner of the *Decatur News* printed a question and then answered it: "What's wrong with Decatur? . . . We are in need of some sort of diversion." His plaintive feeling about local activity may have resulted from failure to observe the many little daily happenings.

Some neighboring communities in Wise County had less activity than Decatur, which, after all, was the county seat with its courthouse and its official offices. At Alvord, for example, many people went to the depot when the Fort Worth & Denver passenger trains went through town, because trains were major happenings. Some of the Alvord people often ran along the sides of the trains selling pieces of fried chicken to the passengers, most of whom kept their windows open during warm weather. The sales were completed quickly, and a passenger was more likely to get a neck or piece of back than a drumstick or pully bone (wishbone), which were often saved for home use.

Just talking to people was an important form of entertainment in small towns like Decatur. When I was young, we had two telephones on the wall of the family bedroom because Decatur had two telephone companies, the Southwestern and the Independent.

Wise County, being west of Fort Worth, was *Star-Telegram*

country, a state of mind carefully developed and exploited by Amon Carter, owner and publisher. Mr. Carter was said to have come from neighboring Montague County, where as a boy he had sold fried chicken to passengers on the Fort Worth & Denver at Bowie. He did such a thorough job of making his paper spokesman for West Texas that we questioned the manhood of anybody who subscribed to the *Dallas News*.

When I was five or six years old, the family was busily preparing to go to Bowie to hear a speech by William Jennings Bryan, a politician of populist beliefs, sometimes called the "peerless leader" of the Democratic party. He had three times been an unsuccessful candidate for president of the United States.

Henry Will and I, dressed in pretty little suits Mama made for us, watched Dad strop his long "cut-throat" razor, lather his face with the brush from his shaving mug, and then shave. The shaving procedure always interested us, and we looked forward to the time when we could shave. Because we were in a hurry to get started, Dad put his razor down within our reach and went to the bedroom to finish dressing. Henry followed him.

Deciding I wanted to shave, I opened the razor and stroked it downward on my right cheek. The blade did not glide across my smooth skin but cut into my cheek. Our trip was delayed while Dad stopped the bleeding with some yellow styptic powder and Mama changed my suit.

The razor cut was probably fortunate; otherwise I might not remember that I heard one of the great orators of the century. Bryan spoke in a large, hot tent, which was crowded with admirers. There were no public address systems in those days, but he did not need one. Everyone in the tent and many standing outside heard his resonant voice and understood his words.

We heard the Bryan speech shortly before Dad raised money from friends, bought a mineral lease on property near Wichita Falls from two wealthy gentlemen, and arranged to use a Star drilling rig, a small, steam-powered standard tool outfit for drilling shallow wells. When Dad got a little show of oil, the wealthy lessors sued to break the lease. They failed in their court effort but added legal fees to Dad's expenses. Dad failed by several hundred feet to drill deep enough, but he was on top of what later proved to be the shallow KMA pool, a great producer.

Dad drove a Model T Ford at that time and resented being crowded off the road by men driving big Cadillacs in the oil-field areas, so he developed a tactic that got him at least half the road. When he saw a big car coming, Dad steered his little car with a wobble, as though he were drunk. His ruse worked.

Mama, Henry, and I lived in a tent with Dad part of the time he was drilling the well. Henry and I were too young to understand drilling procedures. We did notice, however, that Mr. Darling, the driller, could wiggle his ears, which we considered an outstanding accomplishment.

It was in the oil fields that I heard a friend ask Dad, "Why do cars scare horses?"

"Well, horses are accustomed to seeing vehicles with wheels being pulled by other horses. When they see vehicles traveling without horses, they feel the way you would if you should see a pair of pants walking along the street without a man in them."

One time when we were riding with Dad in his Model T we saw a big tarantula on a narrow dirt road bordered with sunflowers. Dad stopped the car, cut off a sunflower stalk, and pushed the creature with it. The poor dumb tarantula attacked the stalk and lost the encounter when Dad impaled it on the sharp end of the stalk.

After the well turned out dry, we went home, and Henry and I were in a wedding. We wore our prettiest little suits. I walked down the stairway at Dr. Ingram's home as ring bearer in the marriage of his daughter, Jewel, and a young theological graduate. I carried a calla lily with the wedding ring on the golden spadix sticking up in the the middle of the lily.

Mama had a passion for keeping everything spotless, including her sons. When she soaped the washrag and scrubbed our ears,

Henry and I yelled so loudly that some of the neighbors may have wondered if she was murdering us. Once when we visited Uncle Newt and his family at Waxahachie, Mama gave us a good scrubbing with a long-handled brush she found in the bathroom. When we learned the brush was the one Aunt Louise used to clean the toilet, we had to get bathed again.

Our concrete storm cellar, the only one within several blocks, provided physical security. When turbulent clouds threatened with their streaks of lightning and booming thunder, we went to the storm cellar and often met our neighbors there. The kids, excited by the storm, giggled while looking scared. Dad stayed by the door and looked outside occasionally until the storm passed.

Women wore hats in the first three or four decades of this century, and there was enough hat business in Decatur for Mrs. Melton to make a living for herself and her sons operating a millinery shop on the north side of the square. She was skillful at making, trimming, and selling women's hats. My mother was a frequent customer.

A fairly common practice in those days was "saucering and blowing" hot coffee, a practical way of cooling the boiling morning drink. Some of the steaming coffee was poured into the saucer for this ritual. Uncle John Chitwood, a resourceful man, had his coffee served with two saucers, one for the cup and the other for the saucering.

We heard sounds in Decatur early in this century that have vanished or are rarely heard now. For example, there is no blacksmith shop near the Methodist church, so people can no longer hear the ringing beat of the blacksmith's hammer on red-hot horseshoes and plowshares. The clump, clump of iron horseshoes has disappeared from the courthouse square. The crowing of roosters and clucking of hens is rare. No school bell peals from a water-tank tower on schoolhouse hill. The chatter of neighbors visiting in their yards on summer nights has given way to the clatter of air conditioners and the muted bleating of televisions behind closed windows. Long ago we often heard the bawling of cattle in the Fort Worth & Denver stock pens by the railroad tracks. They were being held for shipment to the stockyards at Fort Worth and seemed to announce by their bellowing that they had a premonition of their fate. Plaintive whistling of steam locomotives has been replaced by the harsh blasts of horns on diesel locomotives and the rumblings of trucks. Perhaps decibels are a measure of advancement.

The movie on the west side of the courthouse square was an important entertainment center in our childhood days and featured the usual thrillers and Westerns, but we liked the serials best. They always ended, until next week, at a point of great suspense. Either Pearl White was being pushed off a cliff or Ruth Roland was standing innocently in front of a curtain from which a big, hairy hand was reaching to grab her beautiful throat. We worried a whole week until we could go back and find out how Pearl or Ruth escaped.

The movies—silent—were accompanied by piano music. The piano was played fiercely for the fight between the cowboys and Indians, rapidly for the cavalry charge, and tenderly for the love scenes, for which "Hearts and Flowers" was often the choice.

The preacher's son told us about his blind uncle who played for the movies in a nearby town and depended on his wife to tell him something about action on the screen. Sometimes she became so interested in the movie that she forgot to tell him about the changes, so he occasionally played romantic music for the cavalry and tender, loving music for the cowboys and Indians. Once in a while the audience whistled and stomped to let the blind musician know he was playing the wrong kind of music.

Uncle John Freeman, Aunt Ollie's husband, was full of jokes and funny stories. My brother and I loved him and thought he was the funniest man anywhere. A man billed as "the funniest man in the world" came to Decatur, a place unlikely to merit such great talent.

[133]

We were in the sizeable audience he had in the high school auditorium. The audience got many laughs from the performance, but Henry sat grimly through the show without a smile. When we were home, Mama asked Henry if he enjoyed the program. He replied, "That man couldn't make me laugh at all; that proves Uncle John is the funniest man in the world!" Maybe he was.

One of our friends, Nielson Young, was in Decatur only during the summers, when he made long visits with his grandparents. He was at our house one afternoon when Henry and I found Dad's fifty-foot measuring tape. Finally, tired of measuring short things, Henry held the case while I took the end of the tape and ran, with the result that we tore the tape out of the case. It was our luck that Dad came out of the house just as the tape popped loose. Without comment, Dad walked to a nearby peach tree and cut off a little switch. Henry and I knew what was coming, but the procedure was strange to Nielson. When Dad stung our legs with the switch, Nielson's eyes looked like big saucers. He may have set a new speed record running back to his grandparents' home, and we would have laughed if we had felt a little better.

If a dog acted peculiarly and ran around foaming at the mouth, word was quickly passed that a mad dog was loose in town. The children, visualizing violent attacks by a slobbering, crazy beast, ran into their homes for safety, and men patrolled the streets with guns. While I do not remember that anyone in Decatur was bitten by a mad dog, I did hear that a person was bitten by a rabid horse.

Once when Dad was in Wichita Falls for a week or two, the Rector family invited us to go swimming with them in a clear pool known as Blue Hole on a creek southeast of Decatur. Mama accepted, and we had fun paddling around and wading on the smooth limestone bottom. The water was exhilarating.

A cloud hung over the pleasant outing, however, because Dad did not know about it and would have disapproved strongly. He

was jealous of his beautiful, young wife and would have been upset at the thought of other men seeing her in a bathing suit, which
she must have borrowed from a neighbor. That was the only time
I ever saw Mama in a bathing suit. Furthermore, there were rumors
that Mr. Rector gambled, which would have raised serious questions
in Dad's mind about Rector's character.

Dad never learned about the swimming party at Blue Hole.
About forty years later I mentioned the swimming party to Mama,
and she stopped me in no uncertain terms, fearing that Dad might
hear me.

In 1923 Dad remodeled our house into an airplane bungalow,
a design popular at the time. Uncle Clarence Perrin and cousin Bert
Davis lived with us and worked as carpenter's helpers to Mr. Chris
England, the skilled carpenter in charge of remodeling. The airplane bungalow, a type of house popular in the early 1920's, had a
second floor that was set back toward the center of the house. Thus,
an area of shingled roof surrounded the second floor and angled
upward from the top of the first floor to the bottoms of the windows on the second floor—the airplane part. Bedrooms were usually
on the second floor, which had plenty of cross-ventilation.

The same year Dad remodeled the house, Henry and I almost got
a baby sister. We went to church regularly, but for some exceptional reason I cannot remember we failed to attend the evening
service on Sunday, October 6, 1923. On that night Dad loaned our
Chandler to Clarence and Bert, who took two young women to
church. When they went to the car after the service, they found a
tiny baby girl in the car. The *Wise County Messenger* dated October
12 reported the event as follows:

> A baby girl supposed to be about three weeks old was left in the
> H. W. Barton automobile at the First Methodist church Sunday night
> while the services were being held, and the little miss was discovered
> by Miss Helen Hoyl and Miss Thelma Petty, who had gone to church
> in the Barton car, when they approached the car after the services. The
> baby was snugly tucked in a large pasteboard box about fourteen
> inches wide and three feet long, the kind that is commonly used by

shoe dealers in making shipments. Several garments were in the box. The little miss was asleep when found, and when she awoke after being brought in the church, she did not seem to object to the excitement among the ladies and gentlemen who had been attracted by her arrival. On the contrary, she seemed to enjoy the surroundings, as she was fondly handled by the ladies. The news of finding the baby spread rapidly and in a short time ladies from all sections of town were coming into the church. No note or letter was found with the baby, and who left it in the car is a complete mystery. A search was instituted in the neighborhood of the church, but no trace of the party responsible for the child being left in the car could be found.

The baby was taken to the home of Mr. and Mrs. R. M. Collins on West Main Street, where she has been given a home. A shower was given for the youngster Tuesday afternoon, and a whole lot of baby things were given to her. The baby weighs eight pounds and is in good health.

Someone said, "That baby was meant for Pearl Barton; that's the reason she was left in the Barton car." We had the only Chandler in Decatur. If we had gone to church that night, as we almost invariably did, and if Mama had picked the baby up and caressed her, as she surely would, Henry and I would have a sister.

Mama wanted us to have a background in the arts, so she arranged for us to take lessons in watercolor painting from Miss Moore. Although we were only seven or eight years old, we have fond memories of the fine paintings we produced, especially one of a white poodle dog sitting up and balancing a cube of sugar on his nose, a picture Miss Moore must have touched up generously. Our happy memories of our masterpieces cannot turn into disillusionment because Dad, in a frenzy of throwing out old things, unintentionally lost our watercolors in the trash.

A few years later I was the one selected to take piano lessons from cousin Emily Gose, who was unyielding on the matter of practicing an hour a day and made me keep a notebook showing the amount of time I practiced. Not wanting to miss any more play time than necessary, I kept the record to the nearest half-minute, a procedure my teacher considered extraordinary. It was hard to practice piano when the kids were playing football in the yard, and it was hard to be the only boy to perform at recitals.

It was during my piano career that Mama became concerned about my hearing because I did not seem to hear when she called me in to practice. She had a talk with Dad about my disability, and they took me to Fort Worth to a doctor who specialized in hearing problems. After administering a series of tests, the doctor pronounced my hearing normal. After that, my response to Mama's calls was also normal.

The preacher's son heard a couple of political yarns he passed on to Henry and me. One was about a man from the Paradise community who had been elected to the state legislature. He was walking along Congress Avenue, on his first trip to Austin, when a newsboy rushed up to him and said, "*Austin Statesman*, Mister."

The gentleman replied, "Why, yes son, I'm a statesman, but how did you know?"

A couple of years later the same gentleman, running for reelection, stopped his buggy near Chico, walked out into a field where a farmer was plowing and said, "Sir, would you please vote for me for reelection to the legislature?"

The farmer, being hard of hearing, squinted at the politician and replied, "Shore, I'll vote fer ye; that sonabitch we got down there now ain't done nothin' for us."

Dad had a keen sense of humor and occasionally took part in a practical joke like the one he and Mr. A. C. Hoyl played on Uncle Steve and Aunt Allie Gose.

The Gose family lived in a comfortable home across the street from Mr. Hoyl's big home, which featured the white columns of a Southern mansion. Several of Aunt Allie's relatives came for a visit and, possibly without realizing it, overstayed their welcome a number of days. Finally they left, much to the relief of the host and hostess.

Dad and Mr. Hoyl obtained a blank telegram form and wrote a

message to the Goses, ostensibly from another family of relatives, stating that they were arriving at 9:30 that very evening on the Fort Worth & Denver. In those days telegrams were transcribed in longhand by the operator after he had recorded the dots and dashes of the Morse code, so the fake telegram looked official. Under the circumstances, Uncle Steve and Aunt Allie were worried about the prospect of a house full of new guests.

The Goses were hospitable but revealed a little irritation when the Hoyl and Barton families showed up about 7:00 P.M. for a leisurely summer visit on their front porch. Uncle Steve seemed restless while participating in talk about family matters, crops, weather, and the like, and he showed increasing signs of stress as the evening wore on. When he finally said something about a telegram and new visitors, Dad and Mr. Hoyl laughed and told him what they had done. Aunt Allie looked relieved. Uncle Steve laughed a little but gave the impression he thought the joke was not very funny.

A year or two later Uncle Steve opened a significant oil field not far from Archer City, and he and Aunt Allie bought an impressive new home on Grant Street in Wichita Falls. Their son Jarrell, almost grown at the time, told us about the new house. We were greatly impressed when he told us, "If you want the maid to come to the dining room, you just step on a certain spot on the carpet under the table, and it rings a bell in the kitchen."

Jarrell, talented musically, studied violin under one of the masters in Vienna. Later, still serious about music, he enrolled in Southern Methodist University, hoping to become a concert violinist. One of his classmates, hearing that the governor of Texas was registered at the Baker Hotel, assumed an impressive voice, called Jarrell on the telephone, and said the governor was anxious to hear him play the violin. Furthermore, the prankster invited Jarrell to the governor's suite a 8:00 P.M. for the performance.

The practical joke took a more serious turn when the conspirator called the house detective and informed him that a handsome young man planned to smuggle a bottle of whiskey into the hotel in a violin case after 7:30 P.M. The house detective was alert and had a plainclothes policeman with him to make the arrest.

The master carpenter who remodeled our home, Chris England, had a house between us and the school building. One night his house burned. There was no fire plug, and the men of the neighborhood and members of the volunteer fire department carried furniture out of the house while the roof burned briskly. The roof caved in shortly after the last man came out. I watched Dad and the others with great concern.

We made our family trip in 1924. Dad bought a new Buick and arranged for delivery at the factory in Flint, Michigan. We had a drawing room on the train en route to Flint and stopped for sightseeing in Kansas City, Saint Louis, and Chicago. We continued our trip in the Buick, which was a touring car with sliding glass panels on the sides to close when the weather was bad, a model produced only a short time. Dad was especially interested in state capitols, and we visited every capitol in the Midwest, New England, and the Middle Atlantic states. We also spent some time in New York City and Washington, D.C. The trip was a great experience for two boys who had never been out of Texas.

We did make occasional family shopping expeditions to Fort Worth, only forty miles away. When we entered the northern part of the city, we smelled the stockyards and had a strong sensation of having arrived. Swift and Armour operated large meat-packing plants there. The odor was distinctive, strong, and unpleasant, but the prevailing south wind usually kept the smell from invading the rest of the city.

We often stopped at Striplings (recently demolished), a large department store where Henry and I were especially interested in the chocolate sodas. Mr. Woody, who was manager of the first floor, was a friendly and distinguished looking gentleman who had been born in the first log cabin built in Wise County. He always welcomed us.

If we had time, we often went to the Rialto, a movie house where a newsreel, a short comedy, and organ music were provided in addition to the silent main feature. The organ came up like magic from a lower level, evidently lifted by a hydraulic system. The musician was seated at the console; he and the rising instrument were glamorous in the spotlight. We hated to see the console sink down into darkness at the end of the concert.

When Henry and I were ten or eleven years old, we were standing in front of the Rialto with Dad when he asked us, "Boys, do you know how to tell a good movie from a bad one?"

"How?"

He pointed toward a photograph of some scantily clad girls in the entrance area and advised us, "If the girls are wearing short clothes, it is a bad movie."

Without questioning his advice, we replied solemnly, "Yes sir."

Dad, a great storyteller, sometimes described movies he had seen in Wichita Falls. Henry and I listened attentively, feeling we could almost see the screen.

Our favorite story, however, concerned the table manners of a family in Sequatchie Valley in southeast Tennessee, where Dad once taught school to save enough money to finance another year at college. He lived with a respected, hardworking family and ate his meals with them. The food was good, and he got along with them, except for one problem. Each member of the family used his own knife to cut pieces of butter and, wanting to keep the butter looking fresh and clean, carefully licked the knife before using it for that purpose. Dad discreetly cut pieces of butter ahead of the family, then he got no butter until a fresh pound was put on the table.

Dad, in an effort to solve the problem, bought a butter knife as a Christmas present for the family. They were grateful and thanked him profusely. Unfortunately, however, Dad's present did not solve the problem; each member of the family carefully licked the butter knife before using it. Dad got no butter for the rest of the year.

A good thing about Dad's yarns was that we did not have to leave them in Decatur when we moved away; he continued to entertain us with his stories for thirty-two years. In January, 1926, we got in our new Buick sedan and drove the eighty miles to Wichita Falls, Texas, on a cold, overcast day. We left our recently remodeled airplane bungalow, our friends, our barnyard, our school on the limestone hill, and our courthouse square. We left a way of life. It could almost be said that we left the nineteenth century and entered the twentieth. I was in the tenth grade and Henry in the ninth, and perhaps our greatest adjustment was leaving a small-town school at midterm and enrolling in a city school.

Although my brother and I left Decatur, our birthplace, we soon understood that Decatur did not leave us. The reactions, attitudes, memories, and personality traits acquired there from our countless everyday experiences are still with us.

Once a year, early in June, on the Sunday nearest Great-grandmother Gose's birthday, her descendants make a pilgrimage to Decatur to attend the Gose family reunion; some come from as far as California and Oregon. They come even though only two or three still live there—one a recent refugee from big-city life in Dallas. The reunion, first held in 1923, still continues. Decatur, county seat of Wise, still draws her children home.

Bibliographic Notes

The *Fort Worth Star-Telegram*, *Wise County Messenger*, and *Decatur News* were sources of happenings and quotations from 1890 to the mid-1920's. Copies are in the Texas Newspaper Collection, Eugene C. Barker Texas History Center, University of Texas, Austin.

All quotations from the Scripture are from the King James version of the Bible.

The early history of Wise County was compiled and published by Cliff D. Cates in 1907 in his *Pioneer History of Wise County*, and reprints are available from the Wise County Historical Society in Decatur.

Much information concerning the Gose family came from *The Gose Book*, compiled by Thelma P. C. Yost, privately published in 1970, and sold by the Wise County Historical Society.

Some information in regard to World War II and the related influenza epidemic came from: William H. McNeill, *Plagues and People* (New York: Anchor Press/Doubleday, 1976); Alfred W. Crosby, *Epidemic and Peace* (Westport: Greenwood Press, 1976); S. L. A. Marshall, *The American Heritage History of World War I* (New York: American Heritage Publishing Co., Inc., 1964); Jerry Korn, ed., *This Fabulous Century, 1910–1920* (New York: Time-Life Books, 1969).

The rearming of the South after the Civil War was described in Otis A. Singletary's *Negro Militia and Reconstruction* (Austin: University of Texas Press, 1957).

Bagby E. Atwood's *The Regional Vocabulary of Texas* (Austin: University of Texas Press, 1969) was used to verify certain expressions, such as "pully" bone.

Other books used to gain a point of view were: Joe B. Frantz, *Aspects of the American West* (College Station: Texas A&M University Press, 1976); Jeffrey K. Hadden, *The Gathering Storm in the Churches* (Garden City: Doubleday & Co., Inc., 1969); Bertha McKee Dobie et al., *Growing Up in Texas* (Austin: Encino Press, 1972); Edward Everett Dale, *The Cross Timbers* (Austin: University of Texas Press, 1966); Ray A. Billington, *America's Frontier Culture* (College Station: Texas A&M University Press, 1977).

Richard Phelan's *Texas Wild* (New York: E. P. Dutton & Co., 1976) is beautifully illustrated with color photographs made by Jim Bones and provides information concerning the Grand Prairie and Western Cross Timbers.

Index